The General Care and Maintenance of
Milk Snakes
Robert Applegate

Table of Contents

Introduction

As a group, milk snakes are among the most popular snakes currently kept by reptile enthusiasts. As a result, only a few milk snake subspecies are still collected in some numbers from the wild; most are captive-bred and have become increasingly available in the general pet trade.

Milk snakes are one of several species of kingsnakes that are very "convenient" to keep in captivity. Their small size, simple cage requirements, easily supplied diet (for most subspecies), adaptability to life in captivity, and great beauty have made them popular with beginning hobbyists as well as with more advanced herpetoculturists. Their bright, sharply contrasting colors (red/orange, black, and white/yellow bands circle the body in most milk snakes) and crisp patterns invariably tend to elicit "Oh!" and "Ah!" exclamations from non-reptile enthusiasts as well.

As of 1988, Williams recognized 25 subspecies of the milk snake *Lampropeltis triangulum*. This number may ultimately vary depending on the particular taxonomic trend governing the field of herpetology at a particular point in time. Many of these subspecies of milk snakes have been successfully reproduced in captivity for many generations and their maintenance has become almost a recipe. On the other hand, subspecies recently discovered or which are very rare in collections, and new color variations which are occasionally turning up, need much more work before their "recipe" for captive care and breeding can be published.

My goal with this book is to provide you with essential information for the long-term care and maintenance of this beautiful and variable species of snake. I have chosen to present this in an informal manner, writing as if we were in the same room carrying on a conversation. Most of what is contained in this book are my personal opinions, based on many years of my own experience and the shared knowledge of others. An additional goal, should you choose to be a part of this program, is to provide you with the information needed to reproduce the species in captivity and provide additional specimens for the public, thereby reducing the need and demand to collect large numbers of additional wild specimens. Besides establishing alternate populations of possibly uncommon or rare species, you will also benefit from being able to enhance your personal income. I am a strong advocate of "Conservation Through Captive Propagation."

General Information

WHAT'S IN A NAME?
Common name
Milk snakes? They don't really milk cows, do they? Rest assured, milk snakes do NOT milk cows. Long before our time some dairyman with a sense of humor must have noticed a milk snake or two in his barn. When he didn't get the desired quantity of milk from his cow(s) he may have remarked that the milk snakes must have sucked the cows dry the night before. In spite of their name, the hard working milk snakes had simply been drawn to the barn while seeking their normal dinner of mice. Even if it could suck milk, an amount equivalent to the body volume of a milk snake would hardly be missed from a milk-producing cow. I have been assured by those who would know, that a cow wouldn't stand still while six rows of needle-sharp teeth were clamped on her teat.

Scientific name
Milk snakes are members of the large snake family *Colubridae* that belong to the genus *Lampropeltis,* making them a subcategory of the kingsnakes (all snakes in the genus *Lampropeltis* are kingsnakes), and to the species *triangulum* which distinguishes them from other species of kingsnakes. Thus milk snakes consist of *Lampropeltis triangulum* and its respective subspecies. In his monograph, Williams (1988) recognizes 25 subspecies of the milk snake *Lampropeltis triangulum.*

The current trend in herpetoculture is to refer to various milk snakes using both common and scientific names though the general use of scientific names is becoming increasingly widespread usually at the subspecific level when referring to milk snakes. For example, herpetoculturists in the course of their conversations will commonly use "hondurensis" or "campbelli" or "annulata" to refer to those respective milk snake subspecies.

Scientific names are used because they standardize, eliminate confusion, and insure one common international language in biological classification and identification. Common names are considered to be too localized in nature and their variation would confuse international communications. Latin and Greek are the chosen languages for scientific names. The standard format for scientific names is as follows: first, the genus, then the species. For example, all milk snakes belong to the genus *Lampropeltis* and the species *triangulum.* If there is more than one subspecies, the species name is repeated again as the subspecific name of the originally described animal for the species. In all other subsequently described subspecies, the subspecific name will be different although the genus and species will remain the same as in the originally described species name. For example, when originally described (for simplicity I am disregarding previously used and

2

Big Joe and Little Harry decide to sacrifice Martha the cow to deter the milk sucking varmints while the herd crosses the milk snake-infested field. Illustration by Glenn Warren.

Sam and Timmy's dad demonstrates to them how baby milk snakes first attack female gophers and rabbits before graduating to cattle. "It's nature's way of population control," he explains. Illustration by Glenn Warren.

Eastern milk snake (*Lampropeltis triangulum triangulum*). This species is still collected in some numbers for the pet trade. Photo by Bill Love.

Hatching Mexican milk snakes (*Lampropeltis triangulum annulata*). This is another popular and widely kept milk snake. The large babies feed readily. Photo by David Barker.

4

revised names) the eastern milk snake was known as *Lampropeltis triangulum*. That was it, two names. Later many other variations or subspecies of milk snake were discovered. For example, the Pueblan milk snake, which was named after J. Campbell, the man who brought it back to science, was described as *Lampropeltis triangulum campbelli*. The eastern milk snake, to distinguish it from the other *triangulum* subspecies, had its specific name repeated at the subspecific level and became *Lampropeltis triangulum triangulum*.

If you are wondering who gives the snakes these names, it is the person who "describes for science" the animal who gets to assign the name and submit it for acceptance to a board of peers. Some snake names mean nothing (that we can figure out), most are something of a description. For instance, *"Lampropeltis"*-the genus referring to kingsnakes-was derived from *lampros* which is Greek for shining, beautiful, and *pelte* from the Greek meaning small shield. Roughly translated, *Lampropeltis* could mean small beautiful shield, presumably referring to the shiny scales of the kingsnake.

Taxonomy is a field which is continually updated as new information is acquired on the relationships between various species and subspecies. There are, roughly speaking, two trends of thought in taxonomy. The "splitters" are the taxonomists who will name a new species or subspecies on the slightest differences. The taxonomic "lumpers" want fewer groups and want to consolidate the existing ones. The ultimate "lumper" would consider all 25 subspecies of the milk snake color or geographic variations that should all be called *Lampropeltis triangulum* with no subspecies. As a rule, herpetoculturists place a considerable emphasis on geographical variants and would probably prefer a standardization of a language that allows for a descriptive isolation of these variants.

Tricolors
Tricolors? This is a term most often used by herpetoculturists to generally describe many kingsnakes and most milk snakes with the ringed three-color pattern. There are many venomous and other non-venomous species of snakes that are also tricolored but most are not popular either because they are dangerous or because of their difficult captive requirements.

Distribution: The milk snake (*Lampropeltis triangulum*) is an American species found from southeastern Canada south to northern South America. The various subspecies inhabit swamps, deserts, and mountains. They live in a wide variety of habitats capable of supporting reptiles.

Origin of captive specimens: Many milk snakes are still being collected in the wild. Some, like the Louisiana milk snake (*L. t. amaura*), are easily collected in winter when the swamps freeze by splitting open decomposing logs above the frozen water line. Many subspecies are collected by the non-habitat destructive technique of "road cruising". You simply drive slowly at night through suitable habitat and watch for the milk snakes on or near the road, or "spot light" nearby banks, ditches, etc. This is most effective during early summer nights. The eastern milk snake (*L. t. triangulum*) and the scarlet kingsnake (*L. t. elapsoides*) are two U.S. subspecies of milk snake which are still commonly collected in some numbers from the wild for the general pet trade. Fortunately, several thousand of the larger milk snake subspecies are now produced annually in captivity. As a general rule, I would strongly recommend the purchase of a parasite- and disease-free, acclimated, captive-produced animal over the acquisition of a wild-caught animal.

Size: As you would guess with 25 subspecies spread over such a large area, the adult sizes of the subspecies vary. Some of the smaller North American subspecies are adult at 18 inches while some of the Central and South American forms reach nearly six feet in length.

Color variations and patterns: Most of the 25 recognized subspecies are remarkably similar, many bearing a theme of bands around the body (with variations in numbers and widths) of three basic colors: red/orange, yellow/white, and black. There is one subspecies from Central America (*L.t gaigeae*) that hatches as a tricolor then turns solid black as an adult. The eastern milk snake (*L.t. triangulum*) looks more blotched than banded with tricolor rings. There are also some unusual color "morphs" being produced in captivity (striped, solid colors, unusual patterns, etc.) and you can expect more unusual combinations to be produced in the future. Some *triangulum* subspecies have been cross-bred with each other, and a few have been interbred with other species and even genera, so expect almost anything to show up on the pet market. I prefer to keep the subspecies "pure" and trace lineage to avoid breeding siblings where possible, although most combinations can make good captives. Be aware that even the scientific experts can't always identify all the wild-caught animals to the subspecific level. If this is important to you, be selective and either capture your own or get yours from a reputable breeder.

Sex determination: There is no obvious sexual dimorphism in milk snakes (external differences between male and female). To determine the sex of juveniles, a male's hemipenes can be everted by, starting 3/4" to 1" past the vent on the underside of the tail, applying gentle pressure with your thumb and rolling towards the vent. This method isn't foolproof, but if you see hemipenes you will know that a particular animal is a male. If nothing "pops" (the process of manually everting the hemipenes is called "popping") you should still use a very small probe to confirm the sex of a probable female because the hemipenes don't always evert with this method.

With adults, a sexing probe will be needed to determine sex accurately. Rather than describe the process of probing, it is recommended that you find an experienced individual to show you how. A snake can be severely injured by improper application of the procedure. Experienced herpetoculturists and sales personnel

6

Central Plains milk snake (*Lampropeltis triangulum gentilis*). This moderate sized (30-36 in.) milk snake is occasionally offered by breeders and reptile dealers. Photo by David Barker.

Scarlet kingsnake (*Lampropeltis triangulum elapsoides*). This beautiful milk snake, because of its small size and dietary quirks, usually will require special efforts to induce it to feed. Photo by David Travis.

at specialty reptile stores should be happy to demonstrate it for you on a prospective purchase.

Growth rate and reproduction: Most snakes grow all their lives, although the majority of their growth will be in the first few years of life. With optimal conditions and unlimited food, most milk snakes can reach adult size and reproduce in two years. Some female milk snakes will start breeding at two years and will continue laying one to three clutches of eggs for the next eight to ten years. Others will also start laying at two years of age but ultimately will become stunted and never really do well or grow to a large size. It would be wise to wait until the third year before breeding your snake.

Longevity: Milk snakes have lived for over 20 years. The average lifespan is probably ten to fifteen years.

Milk Snake Subspecies

Common Name	Scientific Name	Origin
Louisiana Milk Snake	*Lampropeltis triangulum amaura*	USA
Andean Milk Snake	*Lampropeltis triangulum andesiana*	Colombia
Mexican Milk Snake	*Lampropeltis triangulum annulata*	USA, Mexico
Jalisco Milk Snake	*Lampropeltis triangulum arcifera*	Mexico
Blanchard's Milk Snake	*Lampropeltis triangulum blanchardi*	Mexico
Pueblan Milk Snake	*Lampropeltis triangulum campbelli*	Mexico
New Mexico Milk Snake	*Lampropeltis triangulum celaenops*	USA
Conant's Milk Snake	*Lampropeltis triangulum conanti*	Mexico
Dixon's Milk Snake	*Lampropeltis triangulum dixoni*	Mexico
Scarlet Kingsnake	*Lampropeltis triangulum elapsoides*	USA
Black Milk Snake	*Lampropeltis triangulum gaigeae*	Costa Rica, Panama
Central Plains Milk Snake	*Lampropeltis triangulum gentilis*	USA
Honduran Milk Snake	*Lampropeltis triangulum hondurensis*	Honduras, Nicaragua
Ecuadorian Milk Snake	*Lampropeltis triangulum micropholis*	Panama, NW South America
Pale Milk Snake	*Lampropeltis triangulum multistrata*	USA
Nelson's Milk Snake	*Lampropeltis triangulum nelsoni*	Mexico
Pacific C.American Milk Snake	*Lampropeltis triangulum oligozona*	Mexico, Guatemala
Atlantic C.American Milk Snake	*Lampropeltis triangulum polyzona*	Mexico
Sinaloan Milk Snake	*Lampropeltis triangulum sinaloae*	Mexico
Smith's Milk Snake	*Lampropeltis triangulum smithi*	Mexico
Stuart's Milk Snake	*Lampropeltis triangulum stuarti*	El Salvador, Honduras, Nicaragua
Red Milk Snake	*Lampropeltis triangulum syspila*	USA
Utah Milk Snake	*Lampropeltis triangulum taylori*	USA
Eastern Milk Snake	*Lampropeltis triangulum triangulum*	USA

8

Developing a Pet/Owner Relationship

Milk snakes are beautiful, relatively small, and make wonderful captive animals. However, many are nervous, jumpy, and often prefer to remain hidden. There are always exceptions, but many milk snakes will not make good pets if your primary goal is to handle and "play" with your snake. The juveniles are especially nervous, sometimes calming down only when they reach a larger adult size. Gentle, regular handling is the best bet if you want to try to habituate your snake to handling. Some milk snakes will not calm down no matter what you try.

Because each is an individual, with different behavioral traits, you should consider the following: There are two lives to consider with regards to handling. The first is yours. If a milk snake doesn't bite you, or defecate all over you or your furniture, handling the snake will not cause you any harm. If, after being handled, a snake doesn't regurgitate meals, continues to feed, and behaves in a relatively calm manner then occasional handling will probably not be harmful to your snake. However, it is advisable not to handle your snake after a meal (as long as you can see the lump) or when it is opaque or just before shedding.

Sinaloan milk snake (*Lampropeltis triangulum sinaloae*). This is one of the most readily available and calmest of the milk snakes. It is highly recommended for beginning hobbyists. Photo by David Barker.

9

Before Buying a Milk Snake

Before buying a milk snake you should consider your reasons for wanting to own a snake. If your primary reason is owning a snake that you can regularly handle, many milk snake subspecies may not be the best possible choice (see previous section on handling). Snakes also have certain environmental and feeding requirements which need to be addressed prior to purchase. There are many people who like snakes but cannot cope with the issue of feeding rodents. Other reptiles would probably be a better choice for these individuals. However, if you are looking for a beautiful, moderate-sized, relatively easily maintained and docile species of snake, few can be more highly recommended than the milk snakes with their shiny scales, clearly defined patterns and vivid colors.

SELECTING A POTENTIALLY HEALTHY MILK SNAKE

It is not possible to be 100% sure of the health status of a snake or its adaptability to captive conditions. However, by following certain steps in the initial selection of a snake, the probability for success will be considerably increased.

The following are recommended guidelines for selection:

1) Inspect the snake and pay attention to its apparent weight. A healthy snake has a rounded tapering cylindrical body, with no outlines of the ribs or backbone clearly apparent.

2) Look at the skin. It should be "full", clean, shiny, and with no wounds, bumps, blisters, or damp sticky areas.

3)) Ask to handle the snake. A healthy snake is active and gives a sense of muscular vigor when moving through a hand. A limp-feeling snake is usually an unhealthy snake,

4) Let the snake crawl through your fingers. Apply firm but gentle resistance to the snake's movement and feel for broken ribs or any irregular lumps or cavities in the body.

5) Examine the head area. The eye caps should be clear and the pupils in both eyes should be the same.

6) Inspect around the eyes and between the chin scales for mites, and all over the body for ticks.

Site of one of the original Pueblan milk snake captures near Puebla, Mexico. Photo by the author.

Pueblan milk snake (*Lampropeltis triangulum campbelli*). This species can be very prolific and is very popular among milk snake aficionados. Photo by Bill Love.

Red milk snake (*Lampropeltis triangulum syspila*). Photo by the author.

A natural intergrade between the red milk snake (*Lampropeltis triangulum syspila*) and the eastern milk snake (*Lampropeltis triangulum triangulum*). Photo by the author.

7) Gently open the mouth (using a blunt instrument) and look for discoloration, "cheesy" matter (sign of mouth rot), or any signs of infection or injury. Look for excessive phlegm or bubbly mucus in the mouth. If present, this symptom combined with others such as gaping or forced exhalations suggests the presence of respiratory disorders or infections.

8) Examine the underside of the snake. Look for scars or discoloration of scales. Closely examine the vent area for any signs of diarrhea, swelling, or crusty accumulations. The anal plate of a healthy snake will lie flat against the body.

9) After replacing the snake in its cage, immediately inspect your hands for any crawling mites.

If the snake is a prospective purchase and there are any problems found, don't even consider buying the animal. It is a good idea, before concluding a purchase, to ask the seller about the snake's habits, food preferences, date of last shed, and anything unusual about the snake. If possible ask to watch the snake feed. Remember that, as a general rule, a captive-hatched and/or raised snake maintained in a clean, sanitary environment will have a much better chance of establishing in captivity than a wild-caught snake. If the snake is captive-hatched, ask if it is possible to see the parents. To a significant degree, the characteristics of the parents will provide you with a good idea of what you can expect your snake to become. If a decision is made to buy the snake, consider having a veterinarian check for internal parasites, particularly if it was wild-caught.

FIRST CLUTCH VERSUS SECOND OR THIRD CLUTCH BABIES

Is there an advantage to buying first clutch animals over second or third clutch hatchlings? The answer is yes, but not for what is often suspected to be the reason. Second or third clutch animals can be just as healthy, large, and vigorous as first clutch animals. The time and season of purchase, however, can play a key role in determining how soon a captive-raised snake will be able to breed. The primary reason that first clutch animals are preferable when available is that you will have more time to grow them, and thus, will be more likely to have them close to adult size by their second winter when they could be cooled for the first time prior to attempted breeding. Second or third clutch snakes born late in the season will have fewer months of feeding and growth available prior to that initial cooling, two winters down the line. However, purchasing later clutch animals this year is preferable to purchasing first clutch animals next year for the same reasons. Because yearling snakes often will not feed their second winter and need to be hibernated, even if still small, it may take 2.5-3 years to grow and breed second or third clutch animals, but they should be larger and capable of producing more eggs with fewer risks than the next year's first clutch animals.

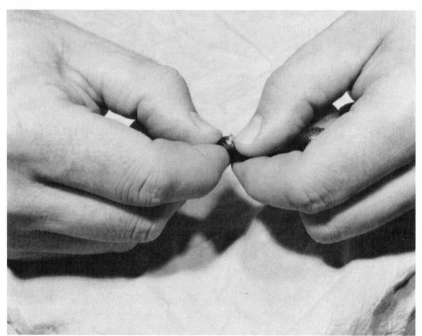

Manually everting the hemipenes of a small snake. It is highly recommended that you seek the advice of an experienced herpetoculturist before attempting this procedure. If not properly performed, bleeding, crushing type trauma and possibly skeletal damage may result. Photo by Chris Estep.

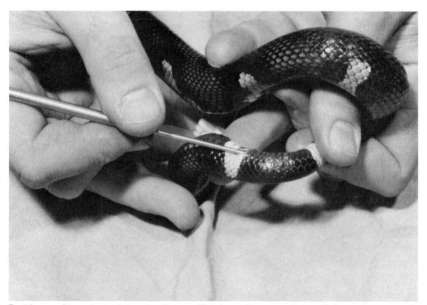

Probing a milk snake to determine its sex. This is another procedure which requires a certain amount of finesse. Ask an experienced individual to show you the right way to do this. This animal is a female. Photo by Chris Estep.

Sinaloan milk snake (*Lampropeltis triangulum sinaloae*). A captive-bred specimen from Cosala stock. Photo by David Travis.

Mexican coral snake (*Micrurus distans*) from the Cosala area. Note the similarity in pattern and color between the Sinaloan milk snake and this species. Milk snakes are considered to be coral snake mimics in a significant part of their range. Photo by David Travis.

Acclimation

ACCLIMATION OF YOUR NEW SNAKE

Once you bring your new snake home, you should set up a properly designed enclosure to accommodate your new snake. If you own other snakes, your new snake should be housed in a separate and isolated room for at least 30 days and preferably 60-90 days. Thus the acclimation period will also serve as a quarantine period.

Initially, leave the snake alone in the cage for two or three days then offer a small meal that won't leave a lump in the snake. Do not handle or disturb the snake for a couple of days after the meal. Three or four days later, offer a second meal. Do not handle the snake until the snake has fed at least three times. The acclimation period will allow you to make some assessments about the health of the snake. A snake that regurgitates its meals may have a gastroenteric disease. If you handle a snake, you have to consider the fact that the stress of handling may be causing it to regurgitate. This can make it difficult for you to assess the cause of the regurgitation. Another thing you will be looking for during the acclimation period is the condition of the feces. If the feces are watery, runny, or stained with blood, your snake may have a gastroenteric disease which will have to be diagnosed through a veterinary examination. As a general rule, it is recommended that a fecal check for internal parasites be performed during the acclimation period.

Finally during this time, you will also be able to clearly assess whether the snake harbors mites. As any snake keeper knows, mites once introduced in a collection can be persistent and difficult to completely eradicate but, if contained in an isolated quarantine area, are easily controlled and eradicated.

In summary, the acclimation/quarantine period will allow you to assess the following:

1. Overall health and behavior.
2. That a snake is feeding.
3. That a snake is not regurgitating.
4. The apparent status of the feces and probability of gastroenteric disease.
5. The presence of mites.

An imported Honduran milk snake (*Lampropeltis triangulum hondurensis*). This subspecies of milk snake has quite a bit of variation ranging from specimens that are tricolor in appearance to others that appear primarily two colored, usually red and black or orange and black. Varying amounts of black may also suffuse the red areas. Photo by Bill Love.

Honduran milk snake (*Lampropeltis triangulum hondurensis*), tangerine phase. This subspecies is the most readily available of the large milk snakes. Photo by David Barker.

17

Housing and Maintenance

Cages can be as elaborate and decorative, or as simple as you want to make them. Obviously a cage suitable for a baby milk snake will be different than that required by a pair of adult breeder milk snakes. What should be considered the basic herpetocultural requirements for any size milk snake?

1) An escape proof enclosure designed for keeping snakes.
2) Adequate ventilation.
3) A shelter.
4) A range of temperatures (establishing temperature gradients) within the enclosure which allows for voluntary thermoregulation.
5) Water (except temporarily when treating a medical problem).
6) Food at regular intervals to allow for growth and a healthy maintenance of weight.

SELECTING AN ENCLOSURE

There are many commercially produced reptile cages suitable for your milk snake(s). They include customized all-glass aquaria with sliding screen tops that lock, glass and wood enclosures with front or top openings, and all fiberglass cages with overlapping sliding glass front openings that lock, to describe a few. With top-opening cages you will usually be better able to control and contain a quick-moving milk snake, but front-opening cages are acceptable. They should be well ventilated. Avoid cages with fine screen sides or low screen openings. The snake may rub its nose raw by sliding and pushing its snout against the screen. Be sure the cage is secure and "escape-proof" as milk snakes will test every possible opening. Check your pet and reptile shops for the latest selection in caging or consult with the supplier of your snake and build your own.

Size of enclosure: Avoid extreme sizes. If an enclosure is too large, a snake can become "lost in it" making it generally difficult to monitor its overall health status and behaviors. A snake in an enclosure that is too large and poorly designed may also stay at one end, hidden, and not venture forth to seek out food items. On the other hand, too small an enclosure will result in a snake that will be cramped, lying in its own feces, and unable to utilize heat gradients. A small cage will also "foul" faster and be more difficult to keep clean and properly ventilated. The proper cage size is one where if the snake were to crawl around the perimeter, it would cover approximately half the perimeter measurement, with a reasonable width to length ratio (no long skinny cages!). A good general rule is a width approximately one third of the length of a snake. Although milk snakes will occasionally climb, tall cages are not essential for their maintenance. A standard 5 gallon vivarium will be large enough for maintaining a hatchling milk snake up to a year. A standard 20 gallon high or 15 gallon low vivarium (12" wide x 24" long) will be a suitable minimum size for all but the largest subspecies of adult milk snakes. Large subspecies such as Honduran milk snakes will require commercial enclosures at least 30 inches long.

Temperature: As a rule, snakes will fare better when they are provided with a choice of temperature gradients. Snakes will thermoregulate by selecting desired temperature gradients. Having temperature gradients with 75°F at one end of the enclosure and 88°F at the other is ideal. In enclosures where temperature gradients have been established, the behaviors of snakes will often yield clues to their preferred temperature ranges or to flaws in the established gradients. If they are always at the cool end, then it is possible that the warm end may be too hot. If they are always on the heated end, then there probably isn't enough heat being provided.

There are many commercial bottom or subcage heating tapes, pads, strips, and devices currently available in the general pet trade that will provide the desired temperatures. Most can be controlled with a rheostat (light dimmer) so you can lower the surface temperature if necessary. Avoid the "hot brick" that plops in the cage. The temperature is too localized and the surface temperature on many exceeds what is recommended and can burn your snake. At the time of writing there are hot rock heaters with thermostatic controls which may be more suitable for keeping milk snakes. Use a thermometer to assess the surface temperature of these hot rocks.

Lights are not generally recommended as a heat source because milk snakes are not usually a basking species. Factors including choice of incandescent bulb, placement of the light, and vivarium design will play a key role in determining the effectiveness of using lights as a source of radiant heat. As a general rule, sub-floor heat is preferable so the snakes can lay over it and warm themselves. When your "heater device" is installed, check floor temperatures frequently and adjust until it has stabilized where you want it. If you must settle for a constant overall cage temperature, 84°F-86°F is recommended. If possible, check with your reptile dealer for the "latest and best" in cage heating devices. This is an area of critical importance in assuring the welfare of your snake and warrants special attention.

Lighting: No additional light is needed if the cage is in a room with windows and indirect natural light. CAUTION: Do not put your cage in or near a window where the sun will shine directly on it. The interior cage temperature can rapidly rise to fatal levels, even with a ventilated top. For display purposes, there is no harm in enhancing the snakes' colors or the appeal of the vivarium design by using full spectrum bulbs such as Vita-Lite®. Remember however, that lights do produce varying amounts of heat, so be certain your light application doesn't upset your temperature balance. Note: Milk snakes should be provided with a period of darkness. This will be difficult if you decide to use lights as the primary heat source.

Substrate: Milk snakes like to burrow. You should provide a layer of sand, small smooth gravel, wood chips, pine shavings, or aspen bedding (not cedar or other "oily" woods) as a ground medium or substrate for the bottom of your enclosure. Some milk snakes (scarlet kingsnakes and others) do better when their cage is half full of dry sphagnum moss. They will hide in and burrow through the moss. When a cup containing baby mice (pinkies) is placed on the surface of the moss, the snakes emerge (often at night) and eat the pinkies. Sometimes this is the only way to get these snakes to readily accept pinkies as food. CAUTION: Some milk snakes have developed a sticky, blister-type premature shed skin problem when kept in damp moss.

Shelters: Milk snakes like to hide and fare better when provided with a secure place where they can be out of sight. Actually, two shelters per cage is recommended, one at the warm end and one at the cool end. Then the snake can be at its temperature of choice and not compromise its desire to be hidden. For example, a snake digesting a meal may prefer to be warm and hidden. If the only shelter was at the cool end of the cage, the snake may choose to hide and could develop digestion problems associated with cool temperatures.

There are many attractive, natural-looking, and easy to clean shelters available from your pet store. You can also use something as simple as a cereal box or small plastic container with a hole cut into it. The diameter of the entrance should be a bit larger than the diameter of the largest snake. Snakes like to squeeze into tight places. Don't use an excessively large shelter. One that is "snug" with an apparent inside volume 1-1/2 - 2 times the apparent volume of the snake is great. If there is more than one snake in the cage, use a shelter that will be large enough for both of them to fit inside, plus one more. Be sure a well-fed snake can comfortably coil inside.

A basic milk snake setup. Photo by Chris Estep.

Large Scale
Housing and Maintenance

BABY MILK SNAKES

Over the years I have tried many cage systems in which to raise baby snakes. A primary consideration should be to keep baby snakes singly in their own cages. Feeding "accidents" occur when one baby eats another cage mate. When they gain some size and "learn" how and when to eat, they can be kept together, except during the actual feeding and for a short time after. If you are going to work with large numbers of baby snakes, simple, easy-to-monitor and easy-to-maintain caging will be a must.

A rack of plastic shoe boxes has proven an efficient and widely used system for maintaining large numbers of baby snakes (see illustration). I use custom-built racks which each hold 160 plastic shoe boxes (clear plastic storage containers measuring 3.5" x 7" x 12"). I recommend the clear plastic boxes with clear lids. It is much nicer when you can see down through the top before you open it. Each rack is built so that, when a shoe box is put on a shelf, the shelf above holds the lid in place. Several 1/8" holes are drilled in the sides and ends of each shoe box for ventilation. For heat, grooves are cut lengthwise in the upper surface of each shelf that will be under a row of shoe boxes, about 4" from the rear of the 11" wide shelves, and about 1" wide. Heat tape is installed flush with the top in these channels. Holes are drilled in the rack's end pieces to allow the heat tape to drop down and heat a second shelf. Each heat tape covers two shelves (20 shoe boxes) and is wired to a light dimmer (rheostat), then through a master room temperature thermostat (set at 82°F). The shelves are then covered with sheet metal for heat dispersal and <u>fire safety</u>. This setup gives you quite a bit of control, and gives the snakes quite a bit of choice. With the dimmer you can increase or decrease the temperature of the warm area above the heat tape. The snakes can move forward to the 1" area of the shoe box in front of the shelf for cooler temperatures, to the rear for warmth. If all the snakes are always in front, the cage is too hot and the dimmer should be turned down. In my system, boxes can be individually controlled in lots of 20, so some can be warmer or cooler, depending on the snakes' requirements. With the master thermostat, if the room heats up, the tapes will turn off, but not until the room reaches a nice safe 82°F.

Inside each shoe box is a substrate of hardwood chips, walnut (crushed) or pine shavings. I have used all with success. A folded paper serves as a hiding place, and a small plastic container with a 1" hole cut in the top serves as the water dish. The water container is wider than the inside height of the shoe box so it can't be overturned. The small hole in the top reduces the amount of evaporation and promotes a drier interior in the shoe box.

One of the author's double compartment cage units. Photo by the author.

The inside of another of the author's snake rooms with double compartment cages, thermostatic controls, and an area with a microscope to assess the presence of viable sperm in females that have been mated and, when necessary, the presence of internal parasites. Photo by the author.

SUBADULTS

In addition to the shoe boxes, I also have a rack of 48 medium-sized storage boxes. These are larger versions of the shoe boxes (about twice the floor space) and can be used as an intermediate step after the shoe boxes, but before the cages for adult-size snakes. They can also be used as quarantine enclosures. All new snakes should go through a quarantine period of at least 30 days, until you are certain that they are healthy and it is safe to add them to an existing collection. This rack is set up like the shoe box rack, with thermostatically controlled heat tape. The shelves are wider and spaced further apart to accommodate the larger boxes.

HOUSING ADULT MILK SNAKES

There are several alternatives to the large-scale housing of breeding-age milk snakes. Many breeders use a variation of the previously mentioned shoe box and sweater box racks, using the larger plastic storage containers which have become available in recent years. With the larger storage units, some breeders opt to remove the lids and construct shelving that allows the top edge of a plastic storage box to rest flush against an upper shelf. Essentially, the storage boxes are used as drawers in a custom-built shelf unit where the upper shelves serve as lids.

What I use for housing adult milk snakes are the double-compartmented, drawer-type cages. They are glass-fronted, of wood construction with a double floor, including the inside of the drawer. The individual cage units measure 24" deep by 18" wide. The drawers are slightly narrower, about 3.5" in height and only 20" deep. The 4" space behind the drawer and under the rear floor of the upper-cage area provides an airspace through which a heat tape is passed. This allows for thermoregulation in the drawer and cage as described for the shoe boxes. Each row of cages has its own heat tape, and they are controlled essentially as described for the shoe boxes. The lights are fluorescent 4' power twist Vita-Lites® (the ballasts are removed and reinstalled remotely to avoid hot spots) set above the 1/8" mesh covered openings on top of the cages. The lights are on timers and also connected to a room temperature thermostat.

The "hole" to the drawer is a raised 1.5" PVC pipe. It extends 1" above the floor to prevent the substrate from the upper level from dropping into the drawer. Coarse silica sand, #3 gravel, and various wood chip products can be used as a substrate with no problems. Avoid any chemically treated substrate like "kitty litter" and avoid the oily woods like cedar and redwood. A hide box and water crock are provided in the upper compartment. Normally there are two snakes kept per cage. During feeding a cap is placed over the PVC pipe and the snakes are segregated such that one snake is left in the drawer and the other in the upper compartment until each has completed feeding.

In addition to the above-mentioned setup, I have a second room with similar but smaller drawer-type cages. The room temperature is thermostatically controlled

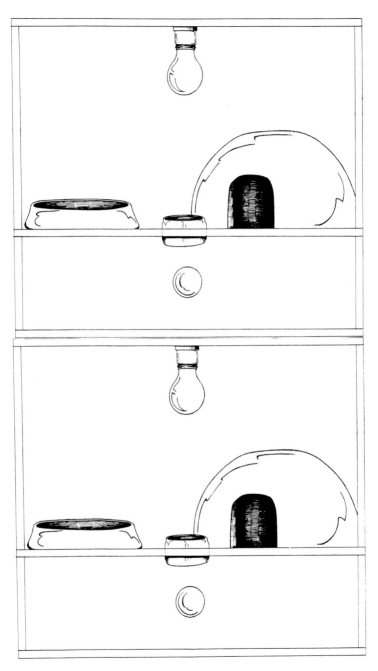

An x-ray view of a double-compartment, drawer-type cage unit. The incandescent bulb in the upper compartment is optional but has been used by some breeders as a source of heat when hooked to a thermostat. Others use fluorescent lights above the cage. Illustration by Glenn Warren.

Racks of plastic shoe boxes used by the author. This space effective system allows one to individually maintain, feed and monitor large numbers of baby milk snakes. Photo by the author.

A basic shoe box setup including folded paper as a shelter, water dish and substrate. Photo by the author.

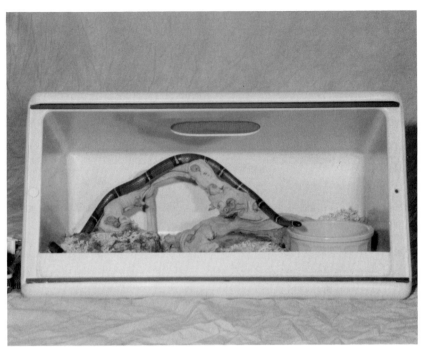

A commercial snake enclosure with sliding glass front manufactured by Neodesha Plastics. Photo by Chris Estep.

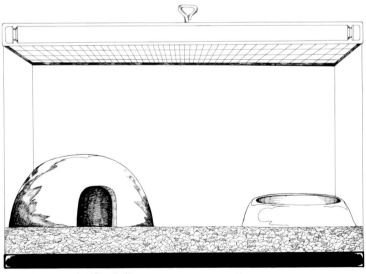

A bare bones setup for keeping a milk snake. The substrate consists of pine shavings. A shelter and a water dish are provided. A heat strip or subtank heating pad should be used as a source of heat. Ideally, two shelters should be used, one over the cool area and one over the heated area to allow a snake access to security. A thermometer should be used to calibrate the heat. The enclosure has a sliding screen top with a pin to keep it securely locked. Illustration by Glenn Warren.

and heated by incandescent lights. The cages in this room, however, do not include any type of lighting. Whatever light is available originates from some natural light through the windows and fluorescent bulbs on the ceiling which are left on and off at random, sometimes for days at a time. I have had equally good results with breeding milk snakes in this setup as I have with the fancy ones with all the timers and special lights. Because of the successful breeding results over many years and other factors known to me, I don't believe that light cycles or special lights are needed to successfully raise, keep, and breed milk snakes. Full-spectrum lights will enhance the display appeal of milk snakes and their enclosures but they are not required for their successful husbandry and propagation.

What has been presented so far in caging will allow you to accommodate large numbers of all ages and sizes of milk snakes and produce hundreds of babies each year. It is by necessity an "assembly line" type operation where one can move rapidly from cage to cage and service the occupants. There are many good cages sold in shops that are perfectly adequate for housing a limited number of milk snakes. You could convert a TV cabinet into a living room showcase for snakes, or a small cage or aquarium with a locking lid will also work well. Just remember to supply the snake's basic needs: clean, dry cage, fresh water, a hiding place, a water bowl (only half filled to prevent overflow), good ventilation, and a temperature gradient from approximately 75°F to about 88°F.

ON NATURALISTIC DISPLAYS

Although I have so far described simple, efficient systems for maintaining milk snakes, you should not imply that you can't build a large cage and design an elaborate "natural" interior with plants, rock piles, etc. Remember, however, that milk snakes are shy and will remain hidden most of the time. They also like to burrow and will constantly "redesign" your interior. A word of caution. Any heavy objects used in a vivarium, such as rock piles and water bowls, should rest directly on the cage floor. If milk snakes are allowed to burrow under heavy objects they may push the substrate from beneath and allow the heavy object to crush them to death.

Feeding

In the wild there are records of milk snakes eating a variety of vertebrates and invertebrates. The preferred foods will vary with the subspecies, possibly within populations of a subspecies, and depending on food choices available, probably from individual to individual. From a strictly practical standpoint, we will focus on feeding milk snakes prey animals readily available to us as snake keepers: primarily commercially raised rodents.

The adults of the larger subspecies of milk snakes can and will eat baby rabbits and/or birds, but most milk snakes will thrive in captivity on a diet of mice and rats. There are some subspecies of milk snakes that are too small to eat a newborn mouse (pinkie) when first hatched. These subspecies are best avoided, or accepted as a challenge, to see if you can find solutions for satisfying their particular dietary needs, at least until they become large enough to eat "pinkies." A good example of this type of milk snake is the beautiful scarlet kingsnake (*L. t. elapsoides*). One of the reasons that this in-demand subspecies is not widely bred in captivity is that the tiny babies are notoriously difficult to feed.

FEEDING SCHEDULE FOR HATCHLINGS AND SUBADULTS

We will start the methodology of feeding with a baby milk snake just after its first shed. Soon after hatching, a baby milk snake can be offered a newborn mouse. It is, however, rare that the food will be accepted and eaten. Normally, a hatchling snake won't accept food until after its first shed, usually 6-14 days after hatching. After the first shed the snake should accept its first meal within two to three weeks. The first meal should be small enough to be easily swallowed, but large enough to leave a visible lump in the snake after being swallowed. A schedule of one feeding per week, with the size of food gradually increasing as the snake grows, will result in a good growth rate.

However, many herpetoculturists are in a hurry to grow hatchlings into adult breeders, so they will often adopt a feeding schedule consisting of offering an undersized mouse three times a week instead of a larger mouse once a week. Three smaller meals seem to produce better growth (more easily digested and allows for ingesting a greater total weight of food in a given time span than a single large meal), and be accepted more readily than one large one. It is normal for a snake to skip a meal or two every so often when offered food this frequently. If a milk snake continues to accept meals, it can be fed through its first winter (make sure to keep the snake warm) and through the following spring, summer, and fall. It can then be cooled during the second winter of its life. The following spring you should be able, following a return to a normal maintenance and feeding schedule, to attempt to breed it.

A shelf setup in which vivaria with screen tops slide. A heat strip controlled by a thermostat is placed in a routed depression underlying the tank. Many keepers place aluminum sheeting over heat strips or heat tape to reduce or eliminate the risk of fire. Photo by Chris Estep.

In this picture, one of the tanks has been removed to show the heat strip. Photo by Chris Estep.

29

As long as they are growing larger and longer you can't overfeed a baby snake. If one should regurgitate, give it a few days rest, then feed it small meals once a week until it gets back on track. With this intensive feeding schedule, babies will usually outgrow the shoe box in the first year.

Don't be surprised if baby milk snakes refuse a meal when opaque. This is normal in many cases but offer a smaller-than-usual meal anyway. Many milk snakes will eat when opaque, but you don't want to offer a food item that creates a large lump in the snake because it might hinder the shedding process. Sometimes when you move a snake to a larger or different cage its feeding pattern will be disrupted. Some snakes are more secure and eat better when in a confined space and don't readily feed when placed in larger quarters. If this happens, you may have to put them in a confined space or back into their previous cage setup to feed until they get used to their new environment.

FEEDING ADULTS

Once the snake reaches adult size you will want to offer enough food to keep up continued growth and body weight, but not so much as to cause obesity. The relationship of food intake to length and weight increases will vary from individual to individual. Some milk snakes will "eat like pigs" and stay slim, while others will not consume as much, but get fat. If the scales are always stretched apart, or if the inside edge of a coil wrinkles or folds when a snake curls up, the snake is probably too fat.

Always keep snakes separate when feeding. If you are using the double-compartmented, drawer-type cages, feed one in the upper compartment and the other in the lower compartment, and cap the access hole. DO NOT FEED GROUPS OF SNAKES TOGETHER IN THE SAME ENCLOSURE.

With males, one meal per week is usually enough during the "warm" season. During the breeding season males may skip several meals (one-track minds, sex only?). Monitor males during this period for noticeable weight loss and review their feeding records. If continued disinterest in feeding is likely to jeopardize a male snake's health, he may have to be moved to a cage by himself, perhaps to a separate room away from the "aroma" of the females before he will resume feeding. If your records indicate a repetitive pattern of extended fasting during the breeding season, you will want to adjust your feeding regimen and offer a male snake additional meals during its feeding phase to provide extra weight gain in preparation for this fast.

Female milk snakes that are expected to lay eggs can be a little on the plump side. Unless obviously overweight, try to offer meals to adult females twice per week. When opaque prior to laying eggs, offer smaller delicacies. If a normal meal is a full-grown mouse, offer a pinkie rat or young fuzzy mouse. Some females will accept food between the pre-egg laying shed and the actual egg laying, even eating a small food animal the day the eggs are laid. It is also common for sexually mature, gravid females to go off feed completely. Offer food frequently because if they didn't eat today they may eat tomorrow. Having something continually digesting is the "secret formula" to getting milk snakes to lay two and sometimes three clutches of eggs per year. Egg production causes significant depletion of a female's bodily reserves and anything you can do to help her replenish them will be beneficial to her.

Stop all feeding of adults two weeks before planning to drop the temperatures for "hibernation". This will allow most of the stomach contents to be digested and eliminated before the cooling period. Because the metabolic rate of snakes slows down when they are cooled, any undigested food can decompose and cause a harmful buildup of bacteria in the gastrointestinal tract.

FEEDING PROBLEMS

Now and then, there is a snake that refuses to eat what we offer it. Most adult milk snakes should already have a feeding history by the time you get them, so what follows will focus on the newly hatched baby snake. By using larger portions the following guidelines can also be applied to adult or subadult snakes.

Before proceeding with methods for dealing with problem feeders, be aware that some baby snakes, for a variety of reasons, are destined to die. They may be deformed internally, unable to digest food, or have some other defects that will prevent a prolonged life. Fortunately, these are rare occurrences.

Before we can expect a problem snake to feed, and before we can tackle the problem, a short review of husbandry is in order. We must provide a suitable environment, preferably a small cage so the snake can't avoid the food item. The cage should be clean, dry, a 75°F-88°F temperature (preferably with subfloor heat with warmer and cooler areas available), have clean drinking water, a suitable substrate, and a secure place for the snake to hide in both the warm and cool zones. The snake should be kept alone and all food items should be of a size that can be easily swallowed without leaving a large lump in the snake. The food item should be left in the cage for several hours and the cage should not be disturbed during that time, preferably with no one in the room. Some snakes are nocturnal feeders, so you may have to try these techniques day and night. Best results are often obtained after a shed, so delay feeding if the snake is "blue" or opaque.

The following is a summary of techniques for dealing with problem feeders:

1. Make sure that all recommended enclosure requirements are provided. Inadequate environmental factors can play a key role in the failure of snakes to feed in captivity.

31

2. Most babies will feed on live newborn mice (pinkies). Place a live pinkie in the opening to the snakes favorite hiding place. If uneaten within a few hours, drop the pinkie inside the hiding place with the snake. If uneaten, replace with a fresh, killed pinkie.

3. Wash a pinkie in soap (non-perfumed) and water, rinse well, dry, and follow steps in number one. The washing removes the domestic mouse scent and may make it more palatable.

4. Get a freshly killed feeder lizard (*Uta, Sceloporus* or *Anolis*) and rub it all over a prekilled pinkie, prepared as in Steps 1 and 2. You may have to cut a small piece of the lizard's tail off, rub the lizard's blood around the face of the pinkie, and put a piece of the tail in the prekilled pinkie's mouth. Frog or worm slime may work here also and is worth a try.

4. Kill a pinkie, cut open the top of the head, smear brain material around the head, then place the pinkie in the hiding place. This grisly technique works surprisingly often, but I don't like to use it if the other techniques work.

5. At this point, if the snake still has not fed, offer it any natural food item you think it might accept, just to get a meal into it. Offer the item (small lizard, tree frog, baby wild mouse) by hand first. If the snake will accept food from your hand, it will be easier to offer two food items at the same time and cause the snake to "miss" its target and to take the pinkie you are holding tightly next to the preferred item. Always leave a pinkie in the cage after a snake has accepted a different food item. Often, the snake will follow the first meal with the pinkie.

6. Remove the snake from the cage, place it in a small paper bag or plastic cup, and try steps 1-5 again if there has been no success at this point.

Usually a snake will have fed before we reach this point, and once it has eaten, it will usually be easy to get it to accept plain pinkies. If it has not eaten yet, heavily mist the cage with a water sprayer to raise the humidity and try the steps again. Don't keep the snake in a wet cage more than a couple of days, and be sure the cage is warm. Another method involves withholding water from the snake for a few days, then put a wet prekilled pinkie in a shallow dish in the cage. Sometimes a plastic container filled with damp shavings and having a small entrance hole will serve as a secure hiding place and encourage a feeding response when a pinkie is dropped inside with the snake.

Note: Some baby snakes react badly to constant contact with damp peat moss, suffering a dermatitis from the acid ground medium. Whatever material you use, keep alert for signs of skin disease when using wet media. The problem may show up as an inability to shed, a premature shed, sticking skin, or as skin blisters. These lesions, when healed, may leave discolored scales or scars. Damp paper towel is a good choice as a temporary, moist substrate.

FORCE FEEDING

If your snake has not eaten 4 weeks after its first shed, you may have to force feed it. Kill a day-old pinkie and gently stick the head inside the snake's mouth, using the nose of the pinkie (or other small dull object) to open the snake's mouth. When the pinkie's head is inside the snake's mouth, gently apply pressure to the outside of the upper and lower jaws of the snake with your fingers and gently pull on the pinkie. This will stick the pinkie on the snake's teeth and make it more difficult for the snake to spit the pinkie out. Wait until the snake is not struggling, gently put it down in the cage, and don't move! You may have to repeat this several times, but often the snake will accept and swallow the pinkie. If this first approach at force feeding fails after a couple of tries, start the pinkie down the same way, then gently shove the pinkie down the snake's throat using a dull instrument. Gently massage the pinkie down the snake's throat to a distance of one quarter to one third the snake's length. If a pinkie is too large for a snake, try a section of mouse tail (the mouse must be humanely killed first). Force feeding sections of mouse tails is a relatively low stress method which works well with baby eastern milk snakes and other small subspecies. When feeding a section (use a section about the length or slightly longer than the body length of a pinkie) of mouse tail, make sure that you insert the thick end of the tail first so that the bristly hairs lie flat against the tail (don't go against the lie of the hair) as it is introduced.

PINKIE PUMPS

If you have several problem feeders and don't have suitably sized food items, or, if you have a pinkie shortage and need to feed many with a few, or don't have time to "play" with feeding problems, you may want to consider using "pinkie pumps". These allow one to force feed small snakes prekilled pinkies. "Pinkie pumps" are expensive but will pay for themselves if they allow you to save just one valuable snake. They can be used to force feed baby snakes assembly-line style and keep them alive and growing until they will accept pinkies on their own or grow large enough to accept larger food items. "Pinkie pumps" are available from specialty reptile stores or from mail order companies.

Most milk snakes that hatch will readily feed on pinkies from the start, so the other "tricks" won't be necessary, but you should have an idea of what to try if a snake won't feed. Some baby snakes, particularly those hatched late in the season, will not accept pinkies until the following spring. Feed "late hatchers" a few lizards or pinkie pump them a few times, then "hibernate" them until the following spring. Usually it is not worth the effort to work with one of these problem late hatchlings over the winter. Snakes lose very little weight when hibernating, and if a snake has any body fat reserves, it will be fine until the following spring. Usually, with spring comes an appetite and a much better chance for easy success.

Shedding

Many animals, including humans, shed their skin. Snakes will normally shed their skin in one piece. If they have difficulty in removing all or part of this skin serious problems and even death may result. Normally, when a snake starts the shed (slough, dysecdysis) process, its pattern and colors become dull with a grayish-blue overcast. When this happens the eyes cloud over to the point where you may not even be able to see the dark pupils. This condition is called by herpetoculturists "being opaque". It is caused by a secretion coming between the outer and under layers of the skin loosening the outer layer of skin. When the skin layers are prepared for the shed, the opaque condition subsides and the skin pattern and colors look normal again. Within a few days after this clearing of colors, the snake should shed, hopefully in one piece. If the snake does not shed soon after the clearing of colors, the secretion between the two layers of skin will dry and virtually glue the old skin onto the snake's body. If the entire body is covered for an extended period of time, the snake will probably die. If parts of shed skin remain, the snake may be able to survive until the next shed, which will probably occur sooner than normal. If just a portion on the end of the tail remains, it will probably constrict that section of the tail as the skin dries, cutting off circulation, and causing that part of the tail to dry up, die, and eventually break or drop off. Snakes do not regenerate their tails, so the animal will be mutilated for life.

As a rule, skin problems including wounds, diseases, etc., will increase the frequency of shedding. Presumably this is part of the healing process.

PREVENTING SHEDDING PROBLEMS

Why does a snake have problems shedding? There are theories suggesting a number of factors including poor health, dehydration, low relative humidity, keeping the environment too dry, etc. It could be one or all of these plus some other unknowns in any given situation. How can this problem be prevented? An easy method is to record when your snake is in the opaque condition. When the clearing of the opaque condition occurs, you should expect a shed within the week.

PROCEDURES FOR DEALING WITH PROBLEM SHEDS

If a partial shed occurs, we should assist the snake out of any remaining pieces. Look for the piece of shed from the head and verify that the eye "caps" have been shed. If they haven't, look for a loose piece of skin attached to the eye cap and lift up gently and pull away from the eye orbit. If no skin is available, use a finger and gently push across the eye, forcing the cap to slide into the eye orbit on one side, but exposing the edge of the cap on the other side. Hook the exposed edge with tweezers or your finger nail. Lift up and off. The cap should lift out with very little pressure. If too much time has passed and the eye caps are "glued" in place, leave them. It is better not to risk permanent injury to the snake's eyes. The snake should be alright, even though partially blind, until the next shed.

For the rest of the body with skin left, pretend that the skin is a woman's stocking. Find the edge nearest the head and roll it back towards the tail. If it seems to be stuck, it keeps tearing, or you suspect that an entire skin is still on the snake when it should have been shed off, find a round-bottomed container in which the snake, when coiled in it, goes around twice. Put ventilation holes in the top, add water to a depth of one half the thickness of the snake, and place the container where it will be 82°-88°F. It may take only one hour or it may take 24 hours, but the soaking and the friction caused when the snake crawls on its own body should remove the skin. Do NOT put the snake in a cloth bag then soak it in a shallow container. The material can soak up the water to a point where it excludes air passage and the snake can smother. It is imperative that shed problems are cared for immediately on baby milk snakes. Within a matter of 24 to 48 hours, they can go from healthy looking to dehydrated, to being on the verge of death. If the snake looks dehydrated (in fact this appearance is caused by the crinkling and adhesion of the old skin onto the new one), don't wait a week after the opaque condition clears, start the soaking immediately.

Perhaps in the wild when milk snakes are opaque they retreat to some moist underground hide-away which prevents any shedding problems. In the wild, a snake can also bask in the sun so the ultraviolet light can kill any bacteria on the skin. In captivity, if we keep milk snakes too damp for extended periods of time, they end up getting skin disorders. However, a temporarily damp cage or a hide box containing a wet substrate, if made available during the shedding process, may significantly reduce the potential for shedding problems.

By closely monitoring your snakes and keeping records of when they turn opaque, you should be prepared to soak them when necessary and prevent any shedding problems.

MONITORING SHEDDING IN BABY SNAKES

It is important that you carefully monitor shedding in baby milk snakes. For keepers and breeders interested in keeping detailed records, a record card can be placed on top of each shoe box. When you see an opaque snake, record it so you can monitor its shedding progress. If it doesn't shed soon after the eyes clear, this will alert you to a problem. Baby milk snakes often have trouble shedding their skins when kept too dry, on the other hand, keeping them too wet can cause skin diseases. If a baby snake has problems shedding, you may have to soak it to help it shed. Baby snakes dehydrate quickly, and this "monitoring system" will save you many snakes you could easily lose to shed problems if you were to wait until they looked dried and wrinkled. I usually put snakes having problems shedding into the cage water dish with a small amount of water (a level approximately half of the thickness of a snake). Replace the lid with one that has only small ventilation holes and leave the snake to soak for a few hours to overnight. Do not place the water container directly over the heat tape area. If the skin hasn't come off during the soaking period, it should at least be soft enough that you should be able to easily remove it by hand.

As a general rule, if a snake's eyes have cleared up and a week later it hasn't shed, you should strongly consider soaking it.

FREQUENCY OF SHEDDING

Snakes shed several times per year. A baby milk snake on a rapid growth feeding regimen may shed 12 or more times per year. Five to six times per year is normal for older milk snakes that are being cooled over the winters for breeding. When snakes are being cooled (hibernated) they still get opaque and they still clear up and shed, but the whole process goes much slower. It may take over one month from being opaque to shedding. If the snake looks dehydrated, then you can soak as previously described, but maintain it at the cool temperature at which the snake is being kept. Do not warm it up to soak and then return it to the cool condition.

THE EFFECT OF PHYSICAL TRAUMA DURING THE SHEDDING PROCESS

If a snake's skin is torn while opaque, or before it is ready to shed, it can be a serious problem. The skin underneath will be sticky and obviously not ready to be exposed. A small area will usually dry, scab over, then after two sheds become scarred. If the skin is accidentally torn, an antibacterial ointment can be applied to the wound. To avoid an accident it is best not to handle opaque snakes.

One of the author's individual record cards. Front. Photo by the author.

Breeding Milk Snakes

The successful breeding of milk snakes is a culmination of all we have covered so far plus some. Breeding procedures for most subspecies of milk snakes can be described as almost a "recipe". The following procedures are the steps of this recipe.

HIBERNATION/BRUMATION

In the middle of October stop feeding adult breeders but maintain normal temperatures until November first. If you live in a temperate zone, beginning in November, turn off all lights and heat sources to lower the ambient room temperature to 50°F-55°F. In warmer climates a different approach could be used to get the desired 50°F-55°F room temperature. Some of the methods used may include air conditioners, fans on timers that allow cool night air to blow in, and finally the use of thermostatically controlled coolers used to maintain wines at the appropriate temperatures. The latter, though expensive, will allow one to cool snakes within closely controlled parameters at any time of the year. Because of the warm weather and high background temperatures of an area such as Southern California, it can sometimes take several weeks for the temperatures to drop to the desired level. This can cause problems with some of the montane subspecies, but does not seem to adversely affect the breeding of most milk snakes. During this cooling period, keep the reptile room closed and try to keep temperature fluctuations to a minimum to avoid respiratory problems. Usually there should be no more than a ten degree variance over a two week period of time. Herpetoculturists refer to this cooling procedure as hibernation, although it is considered more accurate to call it "brumation", based on the most recent research. Most reptiles don't hibernate in the true sense because, even though their metabolism has slowed considerably, they can perform various levels of activity such as drinking and moving about.

However, the word brumation elicits associations that do not really fit from a herpetocultural point of view. Indeed, brumation has not been widely adopted by the herpetocultural community and will probably not be. It is a word that looks and sounds wrong. The closest word to it in most people's memory is ruminate (not "brume", meaning winter from which it was derived). Brumate and brumation in terms of popular use simply do not work. It would make much more sense to expand the definitions of hibernation and hibernate to include the following:

---

hibernation: 1. a popular term used by herpetoculturists in reference to the winter cooling of amphibians and reptiles in captivity usually associated with reduced activity and fasting. 2. the process of being subject to reduced winter temperatures and the associated reduced activity and fasting (used with amphibians and reptiles in the reference of herpetoculture).

Mexican milk snake (*Lampropeltis triangulum annulata*) laying eggs. Photo by the author.

The author's incubator with egg containers. Photo by the author.

to **hibernate:** 1. a popular term used by herpetoculturists in reference to establishing environmental conditions and exposing amphibians and reptiles to environmental conditions leading to hibernation. 2. a herpetocultural term meaning to undergo the process of hibernation with reference to amphibians and reptiles in captivity.

The above is a position that has been developed and adopted by both the author and the publisher. The terms hibernation and hibernate will be used in the rest of the text in reference to the above definitions.

Standard maintenance procedures during this cooling period consist of changing the water once a week, regularly cleaning up any defecations, checking for sheds and shedding problems, and recording anything of note.

RETURN TO NORMAL MAINTENANCE

On March 1, turn the heat/lights back on and provide temperature gradients that offer higher temperature areas, but have a background temperature of 80°F. Within one week start feeding and begin introducing and keeping pairs together at least one day per week for mating. Most of the milk snakes will shed at least once, some twice, after hibernation. A female ready to breed shortly after her first or second post hibernation shed has a scent which is often highly arousing to males ready to breed. Some of the subspecies routinely breed early in the season, some quite a bit later. Some individuals will breed at different times than is considered "normal" for the subspecies, so watch each snake carefully, even if you don't expect anything at that time. Sometimes you can feel or see developing ovarian follicles in a snake. To feel for these follicles let the snake crawl between your forefinger and thumb. Starting about mid-body, gently push your thumb up on the ventral surface until the ventral surface is pushed up into the rib cage. As she crawls (if you try to slide your hand she may tighten up her muscles and you won't be able to feel the follicles) over your thumb you may feel a succession of round "bumps" evenly spaced. They sometimes feel like those old "Pop Beads" jewelry. If these hard follicles are present you can safely suspect she is ready to breed, has just bred, or will be ready to do so very soon. A follicle is the part of the ovary where eggs develop. It breaks open and releases the egg to be fertilized at a later point in time. Be sure to have a male with her at this time.

Copulation times also vary greatly with the subspecies of milk snake. Some are "quickies" averaging 10 minutes, some go well over two hours. In many, the male will bite the head or neck of the female. Most milk snakes will accept multiple "lovers", so it doesn't hurt to introduce a second male and try again. You don't want to miss providing good sperm to a receptive female that has developed follicles, or you may end up with infertile eggs (slugs). Unless you need the male elsewhere, leave him with "his" females. The more matings over a period of time, the better your chances for a good clutch of eggs.

Try to leave the "male of record" with "his" females, or at least have him visit them for a day or two each week. There are theories that suggest the first matings may stimulate follicle development, and later matings or retained sperm actually fertilize the eggs. Sperm can be retained by a female milk snake which she can use to fertilize her eggs even one year later. However, there seems to be a relationship whereby the longer the period of time between copulation and egg laying, the greater the percentage of infertile eggs that will occur. Preferably, there should be a fresh "batch" of sperm available for each new group of follicles to be fertilized.

When the female is visibly swelled with eggs (the rear third of her body becomes quite distended) and becomes opaque, record it (see Records) and remove all cage mates. Prepare and introduce an "egg laying box" which can be any type of container that is large enough to comfortably hold the female, but small enough for her to feel confined and secure. The egg laying box should have an access hole large enough for her to easily slip through. It should also be about half filled with loosely packed damp (not dripping) sphagnum moss. As a rule, female milk snakes will select this specially designed container as the egg laying site. I have never had a milk snake choose the water bowl over the egg laying box for egg laying, but just in case, you may want to remove the water bowl, or lower the water level to 1/8"- 1/4" depth, just enough for a drink, to play it safe. Some breeders choose to remove the snake from her cage and place her in a special cage or 5 gallon bucket partially filled with damp moss and sealed by a secure lid (with holes for air exchange). After her "pre-egg laying" shed (see Feeding for the recommended food regimen during this time), record the date then wait 6-10 days (varies with the subspecies) for the eggs to be laid. If you use an opaque plastic food storage container, you will be able to see the eggs through the container and won't have to keep disturbing the snake.

Once the eggs are laid, check the female for retained eggs. If all appears well (she appears healthy and still has good body weight) then offer her several smaller food items. Within three days, put the male back in with her and try for a second or third clutch of eggs. It is preferable during this time to avoid feeding a female a large food item because when a male starts chasing her around to breed with her, she may regurgitate. If the same volume of food is consumed during this time but in smaller portions (i.e., several fuzzy or just-weaned mice instead of larger mice), she will normally hold her food down. When double clutching or triple clutching a female, it is a good idea to try to use the same snake who fathered the first clutch so that there will be no doubt about which snake fathered subsequent clutches. Because of retained sperm and delayed fertilization there could be questions as to which snake actually fathered a particular clutch.

This procedure of collecting the eggs and feeding can go on as long as the females are willing and able to produce eggs. Most subspecies of milk snakes will produce two clutches of eggs in a season. One type of milk snake, the Pueblan milk snake,

Honduran milk snakes hatching. Photo by the author.

Sinaloan milk snakes hatching. Photo by the author.

routinely produces three clutches in one season. By late summer (Aug.-Sept.), female milk snakes have usually stopped producing eggs. It then becomes important to feed them enough so that they regain their prime weight prior to hibernation. Again, your records and the general condition and appearance of the snake will help you determine if you meet this goal. Don't overlook the males at this time. It is easy to miss a seasonal weight loss in the males as we don't pay as much attention to them. This brings us to mid-October where we start the cycle again!

You may not have to hibernate all milk snakes; a slight winter cooling will work with some. The above methods have been used successfully with milk snakes that are found from Texas to Central America.

AGE AND ITS RELATION TO BREEDING AND FECUNDITY: THE IMPORTANCE OF LONG TERM PLANNING

The average female milk snake will stop producing viable eggs at about 10 years of age. If it is important for you to produce a consistent number of babies each year, you need to take this age factor into consideration in your long term planning. When your female is 6-7 years old you should hold back or buy a baby female to grow up as her replacement. Males will perform slightly longer than females, but 10 years is a good general rule with them as well. You should also hold back or buy male babies so there will always be young "studs" capable of servicing several females.

DIVERSIFYING YOUR GENE POOL

Every so often try to "trade out" or buy babies of known origin from other milk snake breeders so you don't have to interbreed siblings or related stock. So far, in snake breeding, there are relatively few examples of the "inbreeding syndrome" (but there are some) associated with reduced vigor and genetic problems. However, the "pros" that are setting up the stud books for threatened and endangered species say it is important to have as much "founder stock" (animals traceable to their wild origin) as possible to prevent the problems associated with inbreeding. This is another good reason for maintaining careful records on the snakes that we keep and breed.

EGG INCUBATION

Hatching milk snake eggs is simple. You need four things. You need fertile eggs, proper incubation temperature, proper humidity, and proper ventilation. How you control these factors can be varied. The proper temperature range for incubating milk snake eggs is 78°F- 88°F with a preferable range of 82°F-85°F. If you are on the cooler side it will take longer for your eggs to hatch. If you incubate the eggs at too low of a temperature, the babies may take an unusually long time to hatch (if they hatch) and will usually be thin, undernourished, and will often fare very poorly. If you exceed the safe temperatures, you risk deformities (if they hatch) or death.

The eggs are also tolerant of a relatively wide range of humidity. As long as the incubating medium or substrate is noticeably moist, the eggs should be OK. You can find all sorts of research about measuring the amount of moisture needed by snake eggs. The nice thing is that a wide range of humidity levels will work. If the substrate your eggs are sitting in/on feels moist to you, as long as there isn't visible liquid in contact with the eggs, it will probably work fine. Without any moisture, the eggs will dry up and die; with too much, they will either drown (such as when laid in the water bowl) or absorb so much liquid that they rupture.

Proper ventilation is easily controlled as well. As long as there is some air exchange, the eggs will live. Avoid placing large clutches of eggs in the bottom of a deep container or jar. As a result of the respiration of the developing embryos, carbon dioxide, in a container allowing no or little air flow, can build up to where it covers the eggs and the clutch will smother. A decaying incubating medium can also produce harmful gases. This is one cause for eggs that go near full term to fail to hatch even though there are fully developed young inside.

AN INCUBATING SYSTEM THAT WORKS

Put the eggs on top of 3/4" of moistened vermiculite in the bottom of a plastic container (such as butter or cottage cheese containers). If the eggs are freshly laid and moist, you can gently pull a few apart so they fit better in the container, but if they are stuck leave them as a clump. Do not cover the eggs with vermiculite. Place this container and 5-7 more egg containers inside a plastic storage box (sweater box) with ventilation holes around the middle of the sides. Add about 1/2 to 3/4 of an inch of water to the bottom of the box with the egg containers. Put the storage box lid on and incubate at 82°F. Record the date of laying and the number of eggs laid.

This incubating system works very well. The eggs will remain relatively dry, but water will be evaporating all around them. The water will also maintain the preferred incubating temperature so that there will be no drastic temperature changes. Every time the lid or door is opened, fresh air will be allowed in. To keep a constant temperature there are inexpensive commercial incubators available, or a simple one can be made with an aquarium or polystyrene foam ice chest and an aquarium heater. Some snake rooms or cages will maintain the proper temperature ranges. Some gradual temperature changes will not hurt the eggs.

WHAT ABOUT THE GOOD FERTILE EGGS?

As simple as it sounds, this is the part over which we have the least control. If you set up the eggs properly and two weeks later the eggs still look good, most of those should hatch. If they mold, discolor, or start sweating, they were probably destined to die, and there isn't a darned thing we can do about it.

INCUBATION PROBLEMS

There are times when a clutch of eggs incubates for over 2 months, then hatches, except for one or two eggs that have died and completely rotted away. These eggs are usually in the center of the clutch and could not safely be removed. As a rule, don't be too worried about removing bad eggs during incubation. If they smell, sweat, discolor, and you can easily pull or separate them, then, by all means, do so. The incubator will smell better and it will help keep the air from going "stale." However, be careful not to ruin a good neighboring egg by rupturing its shell while trying to pry out a bad egg. Try to leave the eggs in the basic position they are found, relative to the top and bottom of the eggs.

CARRION FLIES

If you are unfortunate to have those nasty little humpbacked carrion flies attack your bad eggs, you will need to take action. If allowed to lay numerous eggs and to multiply in your incubator, they can and will kill good eggs, particularly those attached to bad ones. If present, you may have to actually wash the clutch in lukewarm fresh water. Use a soft brush to remove fly eggs, and change the egg substrate to rid yourself of these flies.

INCUBATING LARGE NUMBERS OF EGGS

When there are several clutches incubating, it is a good idea to stack the incubating boxes in sequence so the box containing the oldest eggs is always on the top. There it will be easier to watch for unexpected hatchlings. When a clutch is expected to hatch, the container with the clutch can be taken out of the plastic storage box and transferred into a smaller plastic shoe box. A very small amount of water should be added to the floor of the box and it should then be placed elsewhere in the incubator. This will allow you to keep exact records of how many snakes will have hatched in a given clutch (container) without the danger of them getting mixed up with others hatching at the same time inside the larger plastic storage box.

RECOMMENDED PROCEDURES WITH HATCHING EGGS

Like most snakes, milk snakes, following slitting of the egg shell, do not immediately emerge from the egg. Under no circumstance should you prematurely force a baby out of the egg. If it has slit the egg, let it stay in the egg for several days if it wants to. If forced out, a baby snake may rupture small blood vessels that

Scarlet kingsnake (*Lampropeltis triangulum elapsoides*). An unusual specimen from Hillsborough County, Florida. Photo by Bill Love.

Louisiana milk snake (*Lampropeltis triangulum amaura*). Photo by the author.

are not ready to be separated from the egg remains, and bleed to death. If most eggs are slit (baby snakes cut the shell with their egg tooth) and a day or two later there are eggs that haven't slit, carefully slit the high point of the egg with cuticle scissors. Cut a 1" long slit, then a 1/4" cross cut at right angles to the center of the long cut, to be sure the baby can squeeze out. You don't want to loose a baby just because it lost an egg tooth or the shell is a little too thick.

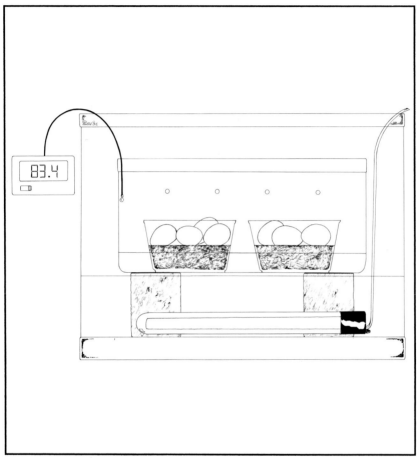

A simple incubator using an aquarium and a submersible heater.

A plastic storage box is placed on bricks above the water. The temperature inside the box is calibrated by using the thermostatic control on the heater and a digital thermometer with an external probe which should be placed inside the box. The cover on the storage box should be in place and the top of the aquarium covered during calibration and incubation. The eggs are eventually placed in containers with a small amount of vermiculite. The containers are then placed in the storage box (with holes for aeration) and a small amount of water is added to the bottom of the storage box. The covers are put in place. A few holes should be drilled in the aquarium cover or a very small opening should be allowed for air exchange. The digital thermometer with probe should allow for constant monitoring of temperature. Illustration by Glenn Warren.

Records

A very important and surprisingly useful aspect of herpetoculture is record keeping. Every snake should have an individual record card. Five inch by eight inch file cards have proven to be a convenient size. Each card should have the snake's sex, the common and scientific name, the source of origination, and a description of any distinguishing marks. Feeding and shedding data should also be recorded on the card. This information can be stored in a relatively small space. The weight of each snake when hatched, along with before and after hibernation, can also be recorded on the card.

On the reverse side, record any disease/parasite problems and dates of treatment. For the males record dates of copulation, female copulated with, sperm check, and any other noteworthy observations. For females record copulation date and which male, sperm check results, date of egg laying, number of eggs that look "good", weight of the egg clutch, weight of the female, date and number of eggs hatching, and the sex ratio of the hatchlings.

Some information on the cards is of general interest and can be referred to from time to time, but other information can be of a critical and timely nature. What is "critical" information? Which snakes need to be bred, which are due for their pre-egg laying shed, and which cages have snakes due to lay eggs.

To keep track of which snakes need to be bred, make a diagram of your collection and place it above their cages. In each "cage" on the diagram put the sex and subspecies (example: L.t.h. = *Lampropeltis triangulum hondurensis*). When mating is observed, circle the female and put a check under the male. As the season progresses you can quickly glance at this diagram and spot any unmated female that may require special attention.

Once the females have bred and are gravid, it then becomes important to know when they will lay eggs. To solve this dilemma, I use a wall-mounted chalk board. On it are drawn three columns of boxes. Fortunately, the milk snakes can be depended upon to shed their skin a predetermined number of days before actually laying eggs. The number of days between the shed and the egg laying varies with the subspecies, but is fairly consistent within each subspecies. Eggs which are laid before or after the expected time frame are usually infertile or otherwise not going to hatch. If you observe an opaque snake that is gravid, put the cage number and her number in column one. When she sheds put that date in column two, remove any cage mates (yes, some milk snakes will eat the fresh eggs of others of their kind), and place an egg-laying container in the cage. Column three is for the date and number of eggs laid. A glance at the board will tell which cages need to be checked for sheds or eggs. A second glance at the diagram will tell who "needs

Taylor's milk snake (*Lampropeltis triangulum taylori*) from Diamond Fork Canyon, Utah. Photo by Brian Hubbs.

A male Dixon's milk snake *(Lampropeltis triangulum dixoni)*. This Mexican subspecies with very limited distribution is not readily available. It is characterized by the extensive amount of contrasting black pigmentation. Photo by David Barker.

a boyfriend". Locate one and bring them together. All of this didn't require sorting through a single individual record card!

There are other variables worth recording which may prove to be valuable sources of information in the future. In addition to the above, I also record the ambient room temperatures, both highs and lows (use a high/low thermometer), on a two week cycle. This seemingly insignificant bit of information helped me solve persistent fertility problems in Arizona mountain kingsnakes *(Lampropeltis pyromelana)* and Durango mountain kingsnakes *(Lampropeltis mexicana greeri)*.

With records such as these you can calculate your cost in mice in raising an individual snake, compare results with different management techniques, see results when comparing the breeding of different sized animals, determine the smallest sizes to safely breed (or hold back and grow one more season), growth rates, egg clutch sizes, sex ratios on hatchlings, incubation times at various temperatures, etc. You can also formulate lots of graphs and charts to use for formal presentations. You may not use much of this information when things are routine and going well, but if there ever is a problem, this type of information will often help you or others determine what that problem is. Over time through the use of records, the trends of individual specimens will show up as different from others of their subspecies and will allow you to adapt your husbandry to their special needs. Remember, with nature all rules are general and there are often exceptions. I don't care what "the book says", snakes can't read. Expect exceptions.

If you are a professional snake breeder, there will also be other types of records that you will have to maintain such as those pesky business and IRS records, but the title of this book is NOT " How to Make a Million Bucks Raising Snakes". Those types of records should be established between you and your tax attorney.

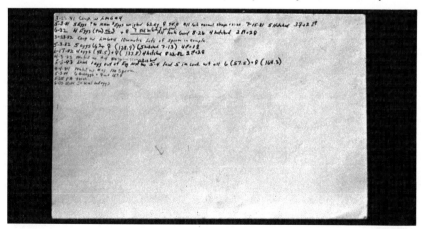

Back of one of the author's individual record cards with breeding notes. Photo by the author.

49

Diseases and Disorders

Milk snakes thrive in almost all "snake acceptable" habitats there are in the wild. That should give you a clue as to their adaptability as a species. If you meet their basic needs they will live a long healthy life. However, as with most life forms, there are certain problems to watch for.

Shedding problems: Milk snakes seem to have comparatively thin skins. Shedding problems are very common and need to be monitored. These problems are covered in the "Shedding" section.

External Parasites: The most common external parasites are snake mites. They are tiny speck-sized blood sucking invertebrates or arachnids. The next most common external parasites in wild-caught animals are ticks. In many books there are detailed instructions on how to clean and sterilize the cage and its contents to eliminate mites. Some areas have mites on their wild populations of reptiles, and no matter how careful and clean you are, mites will find there way in.

The obvious first step in preventing mite infestations is prevention by quarantining any new snake in a separate room from where a collection is kept. During the quarantine period (3-4 weeks minimum is recommended) you will be able to assess the health status of your new snake including the presence of mites. If mites are present the simplest treatment is to place in the equivalent of a ten or twenty gallon enclosure a 1/2 in. x 2 in. section of a No Pest® or similar type of insecticidal strip containing Vapona®. Place the No Pest® section in a container such as a deli container with holes. Partially cover the top or side openings of the enclosure leaving only a small opening for airflow. Leave for 12 hours. The snake enclosure should then be thoroughly wiped and disinfected with a 5% bleach solution as should any cage furnishings. Repeat the process in 2 weeks. If you have a widespread mite problem in your snake room, then buy a Vapona® pest strip and hang it in the center of the room. (Some states don't allow the sale of insectidal strips. However, they can be ordered by mail from reptile specialty stores.) Close off or reduce any air circulation (close door of room and windows and any air conditioning or exhaust systems) for a few days and the mites should all die. Remove the strip in a few days once you have assessed that all the mites appear dead. Repeat the treatment two or three weeks later. Do not leave the strip in the room on a year-round basis. Remember that when treating mites, if you miss a few eggs or one gravid mite, the problem will eventually return.

WARNING: The use of Vapona® impregnated strips can kill cricket and mealworm colonies and may adversely affect some lizards. If the snakes can't be isolated, experiment with small pieces of insectidal strip in each snake cage. Some literature suggests that this application of Vapona® vapor can kill lung worms also. Follow the label on the package concerning use around human and food areas for safety.

Jalisco milk snake (*Lampropeltis triangulum arcifera*) from the Lake Chapala region. Photo by the author.

Guatemalan milk snake (*Lampropeltis triangulum abnorma*). Photo by Bill Love.

Sinaloan milk snake. An aberrant captive-bred specimen from Cosala stock. Photo by David Travis.

Pueblan milk snake (*Lampropeltis triangulum campbelli*). A red-backed aberrant specimen. Photo by the author.

TICKS

Most ticks will be killed by using the same treatment as used for mites. The easiest way to contend with ticks, however, is to apply rubbing alcohol on the tick body using a cotton swab. After 5 to 10 minutes, the tick can easily be pulled off using round-nosed tweezers.

INTERNAL PARASITES

Wild milk snakes can harbor a multitude of internal parasites including worms and protozoa, some of which haven't been identified. Captive-hatched animals are usually clean (a lot depends on the husbandry of your breeder/supplier), but sometimes can be infested with worms.

A common parasite is the flagellate protozoan *Trichomonas* (those things you see crazily swimming around in random patterns when you are looking for the serpentine swimming motion of sperm). *Trichomonas* are easy to eliminate. Metronidazole (Flagyl-Searle Labs) can be safely administered orally at a dosage of 50 mg/kg (2.2 lbs) to eliminate them. A fresh stool sample should be taken to a vet for analysis for new snakes or ones you suspect have internal parasites. Caution: Milk snakes can react negatively to higher doses of metronidazole than can be tolerated by other snake and reptile species.

Treatment for worms includes the use of Panacur® (Fenbendazole) given orally at a dose of 100 mg/kg.

Other Internal Parasites: Herpetoculturally we live in exciting times. Our animals are a valuable commodity which the veterinary community has recognized. They have been, and are currently doing research into veterinary reptile care. In the "old days" we tried to treat our reptiles by ourselves. Failing to find a cure, we desperately took our almost dead snake to a veterinarian. If they would even look at it, he or she would disappear into the back room, pull a reference book off the shelf, thumb to the reptile chapter, and try to match the problem with one of the cures given. Usually we returned home with a dead snake and a vet bill that exceeded the value of the snake when it was healthy. Not so anymore!!

If you suspect internal parasites but can't identify them, you will need the help of a veterinarian, so let him or her suggest the latest and best treatment. If you are advanced enough to identify the problem, you will probably be informed on the latest treatment. An important reference book with regards to reptile parasites and diseases is *Reptile Care* by Frederic Frye (1991, T.F.H.). *Understanding Reptile Parasites* by Roger Klingenberg is an inexpensive, user-friendly book which will be available from Advanced Vivarium Systems in December of 1992.

MOUTH ROT/STOMATITIS

This disease is not common in milk snakes. The earliest symptoms are small reddish spots along the gum line often accompanied with some excess mucus. In time, particularly if the snake is stressed, these symptoms may develop into full fledged mouth rot with the accompanying accumulations of whitish "cheesy" matter along the gum and teeth line. Without opening the mouth, one sign of this disease is when a snake's mouth just doesn't close right, leaving a small, barely visible asymmetrical gap between the two jaws. Untreated this infection will ultimately affect the bone and kill the snake. Fortunately it is easily treated when recognized early on. Daily applications of hydrogen peroxide, Listerine®, or Neosporin® with a cotton swab will clear the infection within a week or two. If severe, with the teeth line extensively affected, a veterinarian should be consulted to administer antibiotics in addition to the topical therapy. Snakes infected with mouth rot should be isolated from other specimens until they are healed.

RESPIRATORY INFECTIONS

In general, milk snakes are very resistant to respiratory infections. However, if they are stressed they may sometimes come down with symptoms of a respiratory infection including "blowing bubbles", inactivity, refusing to feed, gaping, forced exhalations and/or excess mucus in the mouth. Examples of stress-causing situations are not enough nutrition (depletion) after egg laying, excessive fluctuations in temperature, too cool temperatures, and/or poor sanitary conditions. With time, these stresses can lead to mouth-rot (infectious stomatitis) or pneumonia. If noticed early and if the associated environmental or maintenance factors are corrected you may reverse the course of the infection by simply raising the temperature in the cage to 88°F-90°F until the snake's health improves. When snakes are sick they often seek heat. The immune system of the snake will also function better at higher temperatures, and it may allow it to "cure" itself.

If, after a few days at higher temperatures, you don't notice an improvement, or if the disease has progressed to pneumonia (gaping and forced exhalation are indicative symptoms), you will probably need a veterinarian to administer antibiotics to save your snake. Sometimes respiratory problems can be caused by parasitic worms burrowing through the lungs (primarily in wild-caught animals). Respiratory diseases can also result from allergic reactions to a substrate or if a cage is not properly maintained, to ammonia gas released by moist waste. Veterinarians spend years in school to learn this stuff, and read and study constantly (the ones I want you to go to do). If you provide proper husbandry for the milk snake and one of your snakes develops a problem you can't easily recognize and fix--- SEE A VETERINARIAN!!

Eastern milk snakes *(Lampropeltis triangulum triangulum)*. Two normal phase and an albino specimen. Photo by Bill Love. Courtesy of Don Hamper.

Hatched eggs attached to bad eggs. As a rule, bad eggs should only be removed if it can be done safely without injuring the good eggs. Photo by the author.

Tangerine Honduran milk snake. Photo by Bill Love.

Jalisco milk snake *(Lampropeltis triangulum arcifera)*. Photo by Bill Love.

Egg Impaction: Sometimes milk snakes, particularly those laying large clutches of eggs, will not be able to pass the last few eggs. Various theories suggest calcium deficiencies and inactivity leading to muscle weakness (the snake is so tired and weak it can't find the strength to lay the last couple of eggs). It seems this muscle weakness is a major problem because when many of the "stuck" eggs are removed they are no larger than those already passed. However, lets face it, our snakes are lazy! They don't do nearly the work in our cages that they do in the wild, so it's easy to see how their muscles would become weak. But what can we do? Run our snakes around the house or yard daily? Take them to one of Gary Larson's snake gyms? The problem is being researched, and hopefully an answer will be forthcoming, but if you find out first, please let me know. We don't have the answer yet.

However, when eggs become impacted there are several things that can be done. If there is an egg near the vent it can be gently palpated out. If the egg is too large, exert some pressure and when the tail lifts, and you see the end of the egg or find the entry to the oviduct (up against the back bone), you can puncture and drain the egg using a large syringe and needle. If there are more eggs "up high," give them a few days to work their way down to the vent. If they fail to "come down", insert a blunt well-lubricated instrument up into the oviduct and try to work the end first to, then past the next egg. Apply gentle pressure on the egg and, leaving the instrument in position as a guide, try to palpate the egg along the instrument down to the vent where it can be forced out or removed by puncturing the shell and pulling it out. The instrument keeps the oviduct from turning. If the oviduct is allowed to turn it can be "prolapsed" and be forced out with the egg, tearing it loose and severely damaging the snake. Another technique is to try to drain the contents from the egg through the outer body wall, using a large gauge needle passed between the ribs. With the reduced size, the eggs may pass. This procedure could contaminate the oviduct with "spilled" egg contents and lead to infection, but it has worked well for many, and the patient has gone on to successfully breed the next season. Sometimes, just handling the snake and making it move around may help dislodge the "stuck" eggs. In other cases, veterinary surgery may be required. As should be apparent from the above techniques, it is highly recommended that anyone inexperienced with procedures relating to egg impaction should consult an experienced herpetological veterinarian. This could make the difference between life and death.

Case Histories

The following are six case histories which are the production records of six individual milk snakes. While I have many records to choose from, most of my milk snakes are still young and actively producing each year, so their "histories" aren't really complete yet. My personal favorite milksnakes, and the ones I have kept the longest, are the Pueblan milk snake and the Mexican milk snake. I have selected six of the older ones which are some of the more interesting ones to present. When you see Ltc #1 that means that it is *Lampropeltis triangulum campbelli* and that it is the first I have kept (either hatched here or purchased elsewhere) to raise as a breeder. When you see Ltc #9064, it means I have retained the numbering system of the person it was purchased from, and that it was an adult when it was obtained.

The accompanying charts show the following:

1. The dates in years the snake has been in possession.
2. The weight of a female just after being removed from hibernation (usually taken about the first of March each year and before any meals).
3. The date of egg laying.
4. The number of eggs and the weight of the clutch.
5. The weight of the female after egg laying but before any meals.
6. The date the clutch hatched (if they come out over a period of a few days I use the middle day as hatch date).
7. The number and sex ratio of the hatchlings. All weights are in grams and a triple beam balance was used to weigh them.

CASE HISTORY #1: LTA #3 MEXICAN MILK SNAKE

The story of "Patch-head." Not wanting to sound like I anthropomorphize my animals, her official title was Lta #3 (*Lampropeltis triangulum annulata*), but because of an easily recognizable "patch" of color extending forward out of her narrow yellow/orange head band, she was nicknamed "Patch-head." Her story illustrates a problem with the "system", and is a shining example of what captive breeding is all about.

Many years ago a friend in Texas, and I in California, shared a common problem with our respective state Fish and Game wildlife regulation agencies. The State of Texas was about to protect and prohibit the selling of the offspring of the Mexican milk snake, and the State of California was going even further with the California mountain kingsnake. They were going to protect it, prohibit the selling of any offspring, confiscate animals, and arrest the possessor of any of these animals after a certain date. We were both a bit disgusted with this development.

Atlantic Central American milk snake (*Lampropeltis triangulum polyzona*). This relatively large subspecies, up to five feet long, is not readily available. Photo by David Barker.

A dark red more common phase of the Honduran milk snake (*Lampropeltis triangulum hondurensis*). Photo by David Barker.

Red milk snake (*Lampropeltis triangulum syspila*) from Chillicothe, Missouri. Photo by Brian Hubbs.

New Mexico milk snake (*Lampropeltis triangulum celaenops*). Photo by David Travis.

My California mountain kingsnake colony represented three generations (two produced in captivity) and several years of work. His colony of Mexican milk snakes were long-term captives and had been producing offspring regularly.

I will jump over the negotiations part, but the result was that I traded a colony of California mountain kingsnakes for a colony of Mexican milk snakes, and we beat the legal deadline by several months! This is how I acquired "Patch-head". She had been wild caught in Texas and had been in captivity "a few years." She had produced several clutches of eggs for my friend. On arrival she weighed 175.7 grams and appeared relatively young, probably four to five years old. I was told she was a small adult when captured. She turned out to be my best producing Mexican milk snake. The following chart will show you what she did.

Year #	Day eggs laid	#Eggs(Weight)	Female Wt.	Day Hatch	# #	Wt. out of hibernation
1	6-29	9 (101.2)	148.4	8-27	4.5	172.6
2	5-17	7 (93.8)	148.7	7-21	2.5	182.4
2	7-31	6 (71.2)	163.1	9-25	2.3	
3	5-1	8 (98.5)	168.9	7-7	1.7	253.1
3	7-13	6 (77.3)	154.7	9-7	3.3	
4	4-27	7 (99.9)	176.7	7-1	5.2	234.3
4	7-12	7 (69.5)	163.7	9-8	3.4	
5	5-7	6 (88.2)	? ?	7-9	4.2	231.4
5	7-5	7 (85.2)	169.2	9-4	5.2	
6	4-27	8 (105.5)	176.3	7-6	4.4	251.2
6	6-15	7 (76.0)	173.3	8-17	2.5	
7	5-10	10 (146.2)	215.0	7-21	5.5	289.2
7	7-7	7 (96.0)	192.5	9-13	4.3	
8	5-5	9 (130.2)	214.5	7-13	7.2	286.0
8	6-25	6 (83.8)	184.2	8-29	3.2	
9	5-1	11 (146.9)	202.0	7-8	4.7	317.2
9	6-29	5 (44.8)	198.2	All eggs bad.		

Total Eggs 126   119 Total hatched 58 males, 61 females
Averaged 13+ offspring per year.

What an exceptional 9-year career! In all, except her first year with me, she had two clutches of eggs. She laid a total of 126 eggs of which 119 hatched. The sex ratio of the babies was almost half and half. Take away that last clutch of 5 bad eggs and the hatching of 119 out of 121 (over 98%) is even more incredible. After her 9th year second clutch she either refused meals altogether or regurgitated very small meals. She lost significant weight very rapidly and became very dehydrated. It was obvious she wasn't going to live so on August 14 (her 9th year with me) she was euthanized.

What a contribution she made. There are 119 of her "children" out there to fill 119 voids or needs that could have been filled with animals taken from the wild. Did she "save" 119 wild snakes from being collected? Probably not, but I am sure she saved some. "Patch-head", what a snake!!! She will be missed.

CASE HISTORY #2: LTC #9064 PUEBLAN MILK SNAKE

This female Pueblan milk snake (*Lampropeltis triangulum campbelli*) was purchased in 1984 as a five year old adult. She weighed in at 486.0 grams. She had been labeled "Best Breeder" of the colony purchased from the previous owner. She was reported to be captive-hatched in 1979. In 1986, during a routine sperm check after mating, I discovered *strongylid* worm larvae in her stool sample, along with a few *Trichomonas*. I treated her with Telemin PM wormer. In 1987 I couldn't locate any *Trichomonas* in a fecal sample, but the worms were still present. (The opposite of what I expected!) These worms caused me to doubt the report that she was captive-hatched, but later these worm larvae were found in animals I know to have been captive-hatched and raised alone. Since the worms and few *Trichomonas* found in her stools in 1987 didn't seem to have any adverse affects, she was not treated for either, fearing disruption of egg production. Later, after some "eye opening" experiences and losses with some other species, I declared war on any and all parasites. In 1989 she was treated with Flagyl® at a dose of 50 mg/kg to kill the *Trichomonas.* On 7-13-1990 she was very underweight after her second clutch of eggs. 1990 was a year I had to be at work on an island eight days in a row every two weeks, so my snakes were not fed properly, nor enough to allow them to regain pre-egg laying condition. Her sample revealed the presence of the "trich" and the worm larvae. On 7-13 she was treated with Panacur® and on 7-15 she was dead in her cage. I feel badly about the loss of this snake. It is one reason why I strongly recommend that you take valuable snakes to veterinarians instead of trying home treatment. I don't feel it was "her time to die", but that she was over stressed by lack of sufficient food and her prolific egg production. The following chart shows her production for the 7 years in my collection. Some of the eggs laid were obviously infertile when laid, but were included in the counts and weights.

Mexican milk snake (*Lampropeltis triangulum annulata*). Photo by David Travis.

Mexican milk snake (*Lampropeltis triangulum annulata*). An aberrant form of this subspecies. Photo by the author.

63

Year #	Day eggs laid	#Eggs (Weight)	Female Wt.	Hatch Day	# #	Wt. out of hibernation
1984	4-22	9(164.8)	302.2	6-30	6.3	446.0
1984	6-12	8(102.8)	254.5	8-17	6.1	+1 escaped
1984	7-31	9(78.5)	262.2	10-10	1.0	
1985	5-11	12(166.2)	311.7	7-17	5.5	487.7
1985	6-26	9(98.4)	276.9	9-1	4.2	
1985	8-19	8(91.5)	304.8	10-28	4.2	
1986	5-3	11(149.3)	306.7	7-17	5.1	468.2
1986	6-24	9(93. 1)	283. 2	9-4	5.1	
1987	5-3	9(98.9)	378.3	7-26	4.0	515.4
1987	6-26	11(147.0)	275.3	9-6	3.7	
1987	8-15	7(93.0)	265.6)	10-27	3.2	
1988	5-11	12(170.8)	314.0	7-25	7.5	458.7
1988	7-11	12(129.5)	228.0	9-19	7.4	
1989	4-29	13(210.6)	325.5	7-16	7.6	535.7
1989	7-3	11(137.5)	280.2	9-9	5.5	
1990	5-10	10(154.4)	356.6	7-14	4.6	552.7
1990	7-6	12(132.6)	305.9	9-14	6.4	

Total eggs produced 172, total hatched 137 (79%). 82 males, 54 females, 1 escaped from the incubator, or was eaten by another species hatchling sharing the incubator before I could locate it or sex it. She averaged over 19 hatchlings per year. The chart does demonstrate that the earliest clutches are not always the largest by number or weight. Not all my Pueblans show this high of a ratio of male to female hatchlings. Copulatory times vary greatly between the subspecies of milk snakes. The Pueblans are one of the "quickies" averaging about 10-12 minutes per copulation. The Mexican milk snakes are much slower, averaging over two hours per copulation.

CASE HISTORY #3: LTC #1 PUEBLAN MILK SNAKE

This animal was hatched in October of 1981 from eggs laid by a female collected in the wild earlier that year. This female produced her first clutch before she was two years old. She had a good growth rate, with no more than average egg production. She died in 1990 at the age of 9 years. The lack of proper feeding in 1990 probably contributed to her early death, although I missed the fact that she should have had a pre-egg laying shed, again because I was required to be on the island. The shed dried on her, she had major problems trying to lay her last clutch of eggs, and she died two weeks later. Here is her record.

Year #	Day eggs laid	#Eggs (Weight)	Female Wt.	Hatch Day	# #	Wt. out of hibernation
1983	6-3	7 (103.8)	170.8	8-12	2.4	236.6
1984	5-27	9 (115.3)	164.8	8-1	4.5	267.5
1985	5-30	10 (129.1)	191.5	8-5	5.5	328.7
1985	9-31	All infertile eggs eaten by male cage mate				
1986	5-23	10 (112.4)	183.1	8-5	5.4	243.9
1987	5-5	12 (162.9)	228.5	7-20	6.5	399.0
1987	7-4	9 (105.0)	196.9	9-18	2.6	
1988	5-17	11 (117.4)	267.0	All bad		403.1
1988	7-13	10 (? ?)	226.8	9-22	6.2	
1989	5-8	13 (132.1)	265.4	7-24	1.3	348.5
1989	7-10	11 (126.7)	214.5	9-16	5.6	
1990	5-10	13 (170.0)	248.3	7-20	8.4	436.2
1990	7-7 thru 7-12	9 infertile 195.8		All bad		

She laid 115 eggs (not counting the last bad clutch) and hatched 88 (76%). Half of the babies were males (44), half were females. Not all Pueblan milk snakes triple clutch, although she certainly was large enough to be able to support the effort. Even with only a few successful double clutches she had a respectable average of 11 offspring per year. Sometimes, as in 9-31-1985, when second or third clutches are infertile, the signs of impending egg laying aren't as obvious as with good clutches. They do have a pre-egg laying shed, but when you don't see the obvious swelling it is hard to tell if it is a normal shed or really means something! She laid unexpectedly and caught me with the male still in her cage. No matter, they wouldn't have been good anyway, but if the slight swelling had been "ripe" follicles, the male needed to be there for fertilization. When the female is about to lay a good clutch, it is obvious, but difficult to describe. She is much more "full" and expanded in the rear third of her body. You must observe your snakes closely and regularly.

CASE HISTORY #4: LTC #2 PUEBLAN MILK SNAKE

This female is a sibling of Ltc #1 (Case History #3). She never really ate voraciously and never attained full size. This example could be used to support the wisdom of not breeding 2 year old animals. However, I could point to many successful 2 year old snakes being bred and going on to a productive future. I would prefer to interpret these results as there would be wisdom in not breeding an undersized snake, but who is to say this snake would have grown larger and done better if held back until her third year? Here is her record.

Year #	Day eggs laid	# Eggs (Weight)	Female Wt	Hatch Day	# #	Wt. out of hibernation
1983	6-22	6(81.9)	120.0	8-29	4.2	170.3
1984	6-4	5(79.2)	139.5	8-10	1.4	206.3
1985	No eggs					162.1
1986	5-26	7(109.2)	142.5	8-4	2.3	204.8
1987	8-7	5(74.1)	143.0	10-19	1.4	
1988	5-21	9(111.0)	147.8	8-5	3.4	213.3
1988	7-27	7(84.0)	128.1	10-6	1.6	
1989	5-15	7(??)	173.5	All infertile		246.3
1989	7-12	5(60.8)	151.4	9-16	3.2	
1990	5-31	7(107.7)	152.7	8-7	3.4	237.1

This animal seemed to be dominated by cage mates (she was caged with Ltc #1). After the 1985 results she was given a cage by herself and there was some improvement in her growth. She died 7-31-90. As explained earlier, 1990 was a bad year for my collection. I was unable to properly feed the collection. I was able to provide a "maintenance" level diet, but did not offer the additional feedings needed to replenish the egg producers. Consequently a number of my best producers either died or were under weight at the end of the 1990 season and didn't produce well the following season. There are many ups and downs in this business, it isn't "easy money". I can't overemphasize how important proper feeding is to the snake-breeding business.

CASE HISTORY #5: LTC #9067 PUEBLAN MILK SNAKE

This female was probably my worst-producing Pueblan milksnake. She was purchased in late 1983 as a 3 year old. She weighed 458.7 grams. She was put in quarantine for 3-4 months, then, on 3-19-84, she was moved to one of the breeding rooms. She was not hibernated at my place, but had been cooled for part of October through mid-December before I received her. She was caged alone, but on 4-16-84 she laid 7 eggs (97 g.). The eggs looked yellow, and although they were large enough to be good, I believed them to be infertile. I incubated them anyway and on 6-25-84, 1.1 (1 male, 1 female) juveniles hatched! I believe this to be a record of sperm retained from the previous season, fertilizing 2 of the 7 eggs. The other 5 slowly went bad over the incubation period and were tossed out after being cut open. There was nothing visible developing in them. She never produced eggs well, even though externally she looked to be in great shape. Despite her heavy weight she was diagnosed as having large numbers of *Trichomonas* and strongyle worms. She was treated with Panacur® and Flagyl®, but her fertility did not improve. In late 1988 she was sold as a pet (I gave up) to make room for other breeders. Here is her record of (non) production.

Year #	Day eggs laid	# Eggs (Weight)	Female Weight	Day Hatched	# #	Wt. out of hibernation
1984	4-16	7 (97.0)	340.5	6-25	1.1	458.7
1984	5-31	5 (63.4)	297.8	8-7	2.1	
1984	7-17	6 all infertile				
1985	4-28	9 (72.7)	394.1	7-10	1.1	503.3
1985	6-8	9 (124.0)	314.2	8-16	2.2	
1985	8-1	4 all infertile				
1986	4-28	5 all infertile				455.1
1986	6-10	8 (102.2)	289.1	8-19	3.2	
1987	5-4	9 (145.8)	374.5	7-21	1.5	570.2
1987	6-14	8 all infertile	342.8			
1988	4-27	5 (50.8)	421.2	All bad		
1988	6-16	4 (32.6)	393.1	All bad		
1988	7-23	5 all infertile				

84 eggs produced, 22 hatched (10.12) for a 26% hatch rate. As far as we know, there have been approximately 30 live Pueblan milk snakes taken from the wilds of Puebla, Mexico. The four female Pueblan Case History snakes produced 301 hatchlings. Ten times the known wild population! Only an idiot couldn't see the positive conservation effects for the snake and its natural habitat. Because of captive breeding (probably over 1000 produced in the USA in 1991) the Pueblan milk snake is no longer rare, no longer expensive, and more importantly, is now available to thousands of people who do not have to make that perilous journey to Mexico to rape and pillage the environment to get one of their own. Parasite-free ones are available.

CASE HISTORY #6: LTC #3 PUEBLAN MILK SNAKE

This male Pueblan was hatched 8-7-82. His hatch weight was 11.2 g. He was kept warm and fed several times each month until hibernated in November of 1983, when he had grown to 261.5 g. However, on May 2, 1983 he bred with female Ltc #1, and on May 16, 1983 it bred with female Ltc #2. He successfully fathered two clutches of eggs at nine months of age and had good sperm count with no hibernation! It gets better! After his first hibernation, from November of 1983 until March of 1984, no sperm could be found in his 1984 mating samples. However, after a second winter hibernation, at the end of 1984, he successfully fathered clutches with good sperm from 1985 through 1987, when he was sold as a breeder to another herpetoculturist where he also did well. Do males need to be hibernated to produce sperm? This data confuses that issue, but I would recommend it for more consistent results.

Final Comments

What is our world coming to? We have government agencies on local, state, and federal levels telling us (or trying to) what we can and can't do with our animals. Their efforts to save the animals "for future generations" need help. Aren't we part of that government? It seems like I remember something from school about "government of the people, by the people, and for the people". What happened to that philosophy? Does this mean if most people don't like snakes then they should be against the law? With all the emphasis on minority rights these days I don't see how that can possibly be. So what do we do?

Don't you just love it when someone receiving salaries from tax dollars (your money) advises other "officials" who receive their salaries from tax dollars or fishing and hunting license fees (your money) that the "private person" (you, who pays their salaries) should not be allowed to sell "native reptiles" for a profit, even if they are captive produced? Are we going to be so stupid as to wait until animals we want are almost extinct or unavailable from the wild before we bring the last few into captivity to save them? The California Condor is a good example. Look at the public (you and me) money being spent to bring the last few into captivity and breed them in captivity (their only chance) to keep this great bird from going into extinction. If, 50 years ago, these birds had been allowed to be kept and bred we would still have enough to supplement the wild populations from captive-bred stock and the emergency, last-ditch-chance mentality wouldn't exist now. It's the same story with some of the hoofed mammals being captive-bred and released into the wild. We should be allowed to take wild stock (in limited numbers that wild populations could lose and still be viable), breed them, and sell the babies. We would pay our taxes on the profit. Those taxes wouldn't have to be spent later to finance "conservation through propagation" projects initiated by "officials" at great cost to us. There would be a genetic pool of many species in captivity available to supplement wild populations.

How do we accomplish this? Organize!! We have to convince the majority that although they may not like what we do, we are harmless to them, and we have a right to exist and to do what we are doing. How can we organize? By joining the AFH and other national organizations who have a grasp of the "big picture" and by joining and supporting your local herpetological society for regional affairs.

A naturalistic setup for milk snakes. The substrate is a fine aquarium silica sand. The shelter is created by siliconing rocks together to prevent any accidents. One of the new natural-looking water containers made up of simulated stones has been selected. On the left are an electronic digital thermometer and a thermostat to regulate an underlying heat strip. Illustration by Glenn Warren.

Source Materials

Frye, F. 1991. Biomedical and Surgical Aspects of Captive Reptile Husbandry. Krieger Publishing. pp. 712.

Markell, R. 1990. Kingsnakes and Milk Snakes. T.F.H. pp. 144.

Williams, K.L. 1988. Systematics and Natural History of the American Milk Snake. Milwaukee Public Museum. pp. 176.

Supplies

A source of escape-proof snake cages:

Neodesha Plastics
Twin Rivers Industrial Park
P.O. Box 371
Neodesha, KS 66757

American Federation of Herpetoculturists

The American Federation of Herpetoculturists (AFH) is a nonprofit organization whose purpose is to represent the interests of herpetoculturists, those individuals involved with the captive husbandry and propagation of amphibians and reptiles.

The AFH was the first organization to publish a full color publication *The Vivarium* magazine, dedicated to the keeping, breeding and enjoyment of amphibians and reptiles. The AFH's primary goal is to provide the information necessary for the continued and responsible relationship between humans, and reptiles and amphibians.

A membership will entitle you to the following:

- A membership with the AFH. An active organization of herpetological hobbyists and professionals.

- A subscription to *The Vivarium* magazine. Six (6) high quality 8 1/2 x 11" issues, published bi-monthly. Each issue contains information on amphibian and reptile field studies, natural history, biogeography, legislative concerns, captive maintenance and breeding, enclosure design, feeding techniques, and veterinary medicine.

- Special Discounts on AFH sponsored programs and merchandise.

Individual Membership in the AFH is $26.00 in the U.S. Foreign Membership is $32.00. For more information write to:

AFH
P.O. Box 1131
Lakeside, CA 92040
* The AFH is not affiliated with Advanced Vivarium Systems